My Mi' kmaq Mother

N k i j

Julie Pellissier - Lush

RetroMEDIA
PUBLISHING

Library and Archives Canada Cataloguing in Publication

Pellissier-Lush, Julie, 1970-
    My Mi'kmaq mother Nkij / Julie Pellissier-Lush.

ISBN 978-0-9781818-3-3

    1. Pellissier-Lush, Julie, 1970-. 2. Micmac Indians--Prince Edward Island--Biography. 3. Micmac women--Prince Edward Island--Biography. I. Title.

E99.M6P44 2009   971.7'00497343092   C2009-905890-1

Copyright © 2009 Julie Pellissier - Lush

The publisher wishes to acknowledge the Mi' kmaq Confederacy of Prince Edward Island and the PEI Department of Communities, Cultural Affairs and Labour for their support in helping to bring My Mi' kmaq Mother from concept to reality.

All rights reserved. The use of any part of this publication, reproduced, transmitted in any form or by any means electronic, mechanical, photocopying, recording or otherwise, or stored in a retrieval system without the prior written consent of the publisher — or, in the case of photocopying or other reprographic copying, a licence from the Canadian Copyright Licensing Agency — is an infringement of the copyright law.

RetroMedia Publishing, Charlottetown, P.E.I.

Printer – Transcontinental Métrolitho, Sherbrooke Qc

PRINTED IN CANADA

Dedication

This book is dedicated to my dad, who through all these years has been both mother and father to me. While writing this book, he told me a story of losing his wedding ring while sorting potatoes a few months after my mom passed away. He looked all over the barn, moving hay this way and that. He went to the house and removed the cracked floorboards just in case his last remaining treasure from his wife could be found there. It was nowhere, and he was really heartbroken for days on end.

One day there was a knock on the door. The farmer, who had re-sorted the potatoes, saw dad's wedding ring wedged in a potato and knew it must have been the lost ring.

Growing up listening to my father's stories in the evening gave me the same feeling he had when his ring was found: happiness, relief and a special connection to what was lost that was so dear. Thank you, dad, for all your stories. You are my home.

I'd also like to dedicate this book to my family and friends who patiently listened to chapter upon chapter of my writing so I could see if I was getting my thoughts into readable words. They are my two little sisters Anna and Renee; my wonderful Uncle Jimmy Bernard; my Aunties Cathy Fry and Susan Bernard; my dear friends Carolyn Sark, Kate Vermette, Mary Kootoo, Eileen Conway-Martin and Nancy Peters; and my Elder and friend, Judy Clark. I really appreciate your words of encouragement and your stories about me when I was looking for inspiration.

I am also grateful to my uncle Keptin John Joe Sark for his wisdom, and my big sister, Chief Darlene Bernard of Lennox Island First Nation, whose leadership, beauty and grace inspire me each and every day to be a better person.

Contents

Prelude

Prelude

Letting the Mist of Memory Settle in My Mind

Some people collect stamps while others collect cards and if they have loads of money, they may even collect cars or houses. I, on the other hand, collect stories. I was around three years old when I lost my mother to Lymphatic Cancer and to this day she remains in my mind as this beautiful, strong, Aboriginal woman, who I wish, with all my heart that I had known longer. Losing her when I was so young left a hole in my life and my heart so big that it has become an ongoing journey to find out who she was, so I can continue my own journey to figure out who I am.

When she died she was very young, and she fought death with every inch of her being but what that meant was that there was no room for her to think of a life for me without her in it. I have long since passed the age she was when she died but I have always hoped I would do it a little differently if my life ended that early. I want to be able to pass on all my memories and stories of the past to my children with this collection of stories. My hope is that they will be able to share these stories with their children some day - little stories of hope in the darkest of times, little stories of love when everyone's heart is breaking, and little stories of joy where there seem to be only endless tears.

These stories are of my survival, and of how the people around me touched my life and helped me to build and hold all my hopes and dreams together for the future.

Parents hold the stories of who we are, who we were growing up and how far we have come in this journey of life. My father is the only keeper of the stories for me now. Many of the wonderful people who came into my life have passed on. Knowing how fragile life is, I feel it is important to give my stories not only to my children but also to any reader who needs to know that even the shortest of lives can impact and inspire people.

Prelude

My mother was a proud Mi'kmaq woman who grew up in a First Nations community on Prince Edward Island. She laughed easily and always showed her cheerful smile to everyone she saw. Outside her community she was still able to hold her head high, even with the large amount of discrimination and racism that could be found, not only in PEI but, in every small community across Canada. Her life may have ended early, but her memory will live on in me, my children and I hope, anyone who has read this book and has overcome the loss of a mother, sister, brother, father, child or friend. Sometimes when we lose someone who we need in our lives, there is a time that comes when that loss can slowly become a celebration of whom they were and what they brought to our life.

I give these stories to my children now, so they will know where they come from and maybe help them with who they are. Every day I hug my babies close to me, laugh with them, kiss them, and I give thanks for the wonderful gift of being able to be here with them so I can watch them grow. I will start my stories at what I consider the beginning, and that is when my parents met and fell in love on Prince Edward Island.

One teaching I have learned and think I should share, came to me from an elder; and it is that people are where they are supposed to be, and if someone comes into your life, there is a reason for it, so you need always to be open. I do believe that this teaching is very true. What it also means to me is that if you are reading this, you are meant to be reading this.

Part One
Lennox Island

Ne' wt

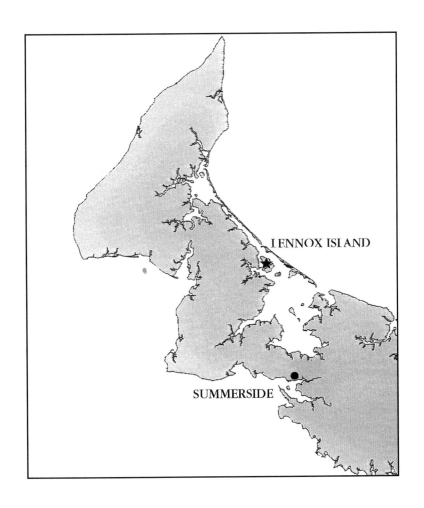

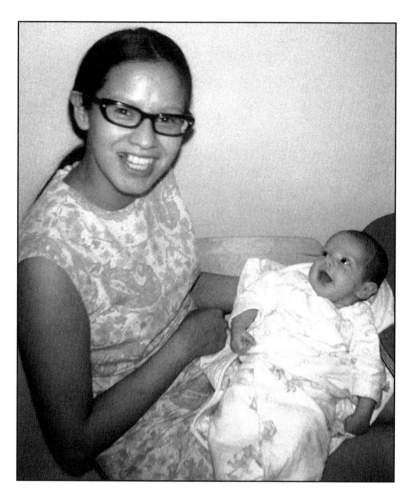

My mother Maggie and me

Who Made Me?

My mother was a beautiful First Nations woman from Lennox Island, Prince Edward Island. She was one of many children of David and Dorothy Bernard. Her brothers and sisters live all over North America and have contributed their strengths and skills to the communities they are a part of as homecare workers, daycare workers, lobster fishers, carpenters and fleet managers. One is even an elder who represents all the Mi'kmaq people in PEI and Nova Scotia. Many share their culture and traditional teachings and many of them take it upon themselves to look after the elders in their communities. Each one has something special inside that they share each and every day.

This makes me think of how special my mom must have been to have grown up with all these wonderful siblings. Her oldest daughter, my sister Darlene, has gone beyond success in everything she has done in her life. She is the Chief of Lennox Island First Nations and performs this role with her power of vision for the community's future. Her commitment to her community runs hand in hand with her commitment to her family. She is a woman who I look up to as a leader, as a friend and as an older sister.

Now comes the hardest person to talk about, when I talk about who made me, and that is my father, my mentor, my daddy, Louis Pellissier. Growing up, he was not only my father; he had to also be my mother after my mother passed away. He was born in Valley Stream, New York and after a few short years there, moved to Charlton, Massachusetts. He grew up with his older brother and sister and as he matured, so did his perceptions of the world.

As a teen, he volunteered to go down south to help rebuild an African-American church that was burned down by a local KKK group. He was never a radical activist, but he always stood up for other people he felt were being oppressed or discriminated against by another group. He was quick to smile and laugh, and it was always one of those deep-in-the-pit-of-your-stomach laughs that made everyone around join in.

What I remember most about growing up with my dad is that if I ever got hurt, my tears became the centre of his universe. He would kneel down and hold me close trying to absorb some of the pain I might be feeling. I always had a feeling of being loved and being safe when I was around my dad.

My mom and my dad are the ones who gave me life and my story starts with them.

Louis, Maggie and me

The Indian Princess Meets Her Sir Galahad

He was working at the Welfare Office in 1969, and he was slowly growing more and more comfortable with this new position. Then, one afternoon, this woman walked in looking for information for her family. She was young and very beautiful. Her long, black hair surrounded her oval face like a halo and her dark brown eyes seemed to look through him to his soul. They took a few minutes to look at each other and they both knew it was love at first sight.

Louis, with his light brown hair lightly feathered around his face was like a dream to her, an escape from everything she had ever known. Soon they were spending more and more time together and he knew that this was the woman he wanted to spend the rest of his life with. Being a white man in her world was a bit of a disadvantage for their relationship but they treated it like a challenge and their love just grew and grew.

Her family was related to the chief, and she had fourteen brothers and sisters who were very protective of the family, especially of the girls. These were things Louis had to consider once they started dating. Her father had an alcohol problem, and would routinely come banging on their apartment door at all hours of the night to tell her to get home. Many times, my father would have to escort him home; sometimes more roughly then others.

After a few wonderful spring months, Maggie began to suspect that she might be pregnant. According to my birth date, I was conceived May

23, 1969. She told Louis he was going to be a dad and it would happen some time in February.

It did not take Louis very long to drop on one knee and ask her to marry him. She was so happy, she agreed on the spot, and she knew she would love him forever.

He was so different with his intense gaze and his light blue eyes that she knew in her heart he would love her, defend her against all others and also be her friend forever. Her life had had many disappointments, many heart breaks and even some violence, but she knew with Louis she would be safe. The Indian Princess had met her Sir Galahad and it was going along just like a fairy tale. True love could conquer everything.

Confused Grandparents

As any good son would, Louis wrote home to his parents that night to tell them the wonderful news. Their youngest little boy was going to tie the knot with the love of his life.

Back in Charlton, Eleanor and Carroll read Louis's words and stared at each other. Didn't Louis write just a few months ago about the alcohol abuse, violence, and even of children running around at three o'clock in the morning in this place? Now he was going to marry one of them and he was saying it was true love Still, being good parents, they quietly sent their congratulations towards the blessed event and wished him all the best. I think there were a few words that stated they would not think less of him if he should change his mind. They both reminded him that he was only twenty-four and if things should change overnight, that would be fine.

They did not know that the wedding that would bind these two young love-birds together was already being planned. It would be in Montreal; not that far away in time, since Maggie did not want to be showing during the ceremony.

Everything went as scheduled. They went to Montreal and were married just before Maggie was three months pregnant. After the ceremony, Maggie told Louis that she did not want to live on the Reserve with her new husband and baby; so once they got back to the Island, they began to look for a little house of their own. She also decided that once I was born she wanted to be a nurse, so she was going to go to school. Louis just grew more in love with her and proud of her strong spirit as her stomach grew large with me.

This was a time just for them, to express their hopes and dreams and tell each other all of their secrets. Louis would laugh at how awkward and large she got near the end, but he would also spend hours feeling the small baby moving around inside of her. Soon their quiet time together would be over.

Carroll and Eleanor

Blue Baby a Week Late

I was due Valentine's Day, 1970. Both thought it was a perfect way to celebrate their love; to have their baby born on this special day. February 14th soon came and went and both soon-to-be parents were growing more and more anxious to see the baby that their love would produce, not to mention that Maggie was very easily irritated at this point.

February 21st was the day that Maggie finally went into labour. Louis was a wreck walking the hallways waiting for word on his wife and baby. Inside the delivery room the doctor concluded that the labour was going to take more time and so he decided to take a short break and take a walk outside.

Just as he left the hospital, my little head began to emerge from my mother. One of the nurses went running for the departing doctor as another got ready to catch me. Seconds after I was born my mother looked up and started to cry, *"Why isn't the baby crying? What's wrong?"*

The doctor came in just in time to see that I was very blue. The umbilical cord was wrapped securely around my neck like a noose and I was slowly losing the fight to stay alive. He cut the cord and soon, I started to cry. It was a sound both my parents would get to know very well over the next year.

First I was given to my mother who was told I was a healthy girl. Then, I was taken outside the delivery room to see my dad. He had been waiting and waiting, getting more nervous, when the nurse came out with me all wrapped up in a soft, warm blanket. He was so happy and overwhelmed that when he first took a good look at his little, blue daughter, he thought my colour was odd, but he also thought he could get used to raising a little, blue girl. Later, when his mind cleared, this became a classic bedtime story for me; so, now that I was here and they knew I was a little girl, it was time to decide on the perfect name.

Julie Ellen

My Name

My official 'getting my name story' went like this. I was named Julie after a very good friend of theirs. If we were Catholic she definitely would have been my godmother. That is how close they were. The ironic thing is that I never saw her even after I was given her name. She remains an elusive, beautiful, blond ghost. Once in awhile, I think of her and wonder what she was like. I wonder if not knowing her made it harder for me to know myself. It's just another one of those mysteries of my young life.

One day I would like to track her down, and ask her who she was and what my parents were like when she knew them. It would be very enlightening, I'm sure, to hear her stories and share in her secrets of that time.

I received my middle name, Ellen, after my dad's mom, Eleanor. This was perfect since we always had such a close relationship from the beginning of my life till the end of hers. It was a strong connection forged further by our connected names. We shared a little bit of each other's soul at different times in our lives.

JULIE ELLEN

Ju'lielen

Colic and the Spiritual Visit

I was bottle-fed on diluted Carnation Milk. Maybe it is because of this that I had incredibly bad colic. If I was awake, I was crying at the top of my voice. We were still living on the Reserve in a very small house with maybe three rooms: the bedroom, the bathroom and everything else. There were nights when my dad would grab what he could and run outside and smash it. He had no idea how to get me to stop crying. Over the long winter months, it became harder and harder to bear.

During the summer, my mom and dad were given a bigger house by the band. They were both happy. It was an actual house for their small family. One night when some of the guys were over at this new house to play cards, they told my dad that his new house was haunted, and that is why he was allowed to live in it. It had belonged to numerous people, including a priest who lived his life out in this house.

My mom was out that night, so once all the guys left laughing that he should have a good night with all the ghosts, he went to bed. My room was upstairs at the time, and dad slept on the couch waiting for my mom.

Sometime in the middle of the night, there was a loud knock on the front door. Louis got up, thinking it was his friends come back to bug him about the ghost, so he ran to open the door. There was no one there. The street was empty; not even the normal stray dogs that roamed the Reserve were around. Not sure what was happening, he went back inside and decided to just forget about it all and go back to bed.

About ten minutes later, there was another loud bang on the door; and then he heard the front door open and footsteps going up the stairs. Well, my father jumped out of bed and ran to the front door. He could see my bedroom door was as wide open as the front door. Up the stairs he ran yelling, *"Get out of my house,"* and when he got to the top of the stairs and looked in, what he saw was me. I was giggling in my crib; looking up at something that wasn't there. Then when I looked over and saw my dad, I started crying which was what I usually did when I was awake back then.

The spirit had left my room and the enchantment was gone. All I knew is my stomach hurt again and I needed to cry. Later it was said that the ghost was actually one of my great grand-fathers, so maybe it was not so unusual that he would come to see me. We did not stay at that house very long either, not surprisingly, with our nightly visitors.

My dad always remembered that he promised to find a place off the Reserve for his new family. Soon he found the perfect house. It was close to Lennox Island but was a fair walk for anyone just to pop over. This would be a much better time for my parents than it had been before.

It was also around this time that a fateful decision was made by my mother. She decided that since she had such big plans for her future, she did not want any more kids at this time. She went on the pill then; a new drug much more potent that what is on the market today. They were still in the testing phase of this birth control, and the doctors told her it was a miracle drug. The repercussions of this single decision can still be felt in our family today.

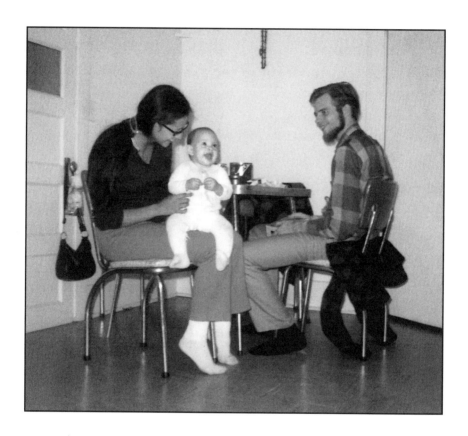

The Oven is Really Hot

Soon I was crawling, and then walking and running all over our new house. One day my mother decided to make some fresh baked cookies for her little family, and carelessly opened the oven door and went to get her oven mitts to pull out the hot cookie trays. I came around the corner and saw the fresh baked cookies just sitting there in the pan smelling so good.

I was about one and a half and I'd just eaten dinner so I still had my little plastic bib on. I reached over to grab the cookies, and then my legs started to hurt as they burned against the oven door I was leaning on. As the edge of the oven door started to burn me just under my diaper, I became disorientated and I fell forward onto the oven door and one scream was all I let out as the plastic bib started burning to my stomach. Mom and dad both came running and looked at their little girl lying on the hot oven door. One grabbed a blanket and the other the keys, and without a word, they started their frantic trip to the closest hospital.

As luck would have it, my dad sped right by a speed trap and soon there were red lights flashing behind the little car. As soon as the officer approached the car, my father whipped the blanket off my still body and screamed that they were racing to the hospital. The officer, in shock, offered his assistance and escorted the distraught couple all the way to the hospital.

After a few hours of burnt plastic being plucked from my stomach and chest, I was sent to recovery where my relieved parents thanked God. Fortunately for me, those doctors took such good care of me that I was left without a scar and with no memory of the whole event.

An Aboriginal Woman Driving?

Living this far away from everything, with the event that had just happened, meant that my mom would have to get her licence. This would allow her to run her errands, attend classes and visit her family and friends more easily.

Back then, she was one of the first Aboriginal women on the Island to get her licence and own a car, so many people would stop and stare at her as she drove past in her little red car.

My father was terribly proud of her. She was now enrolled in her nursing course and life was perfect. I was out of my colic and had recovered without a trace of trauma from my ordeal with the stove. It became another year of peace for the young married couple.

Checking out mom's car

Hot Baths and Lemon Meringue Pie

My mom loved to make my dad his favourite pie and that was Lemon Meringue. It is easy to picture this beautiful Aboriginal woman making a pie and waiting with anticipation for her husband who she loved so much, to come home and be so happy with her thoughtfulness that he would pull her into his arms and kiss her.

Of course, life was not all romance. There were a few fights too. One in particular stands out. They were screaming at each other and then out of the blue, my mother's background of having nine big brothers kicked in and POW, my dad got a right hook straight to his jaw that sent him to the floor. My mother's jaw dropped as she looked at what she had done, and the fight was done then and there. All that was left was the making up and the admiration of a really strong right hook

Many a time my dad would come home and my mom was participating in her favourite pastime of lying in a hot bath with a bottle of wine. How could life be better for them? She was a hard working student and he was still working with the band as the welfare officer. Their future seemed bright.

Fainting and What it Meant

One day my mom was just walking around the house when all of a sudden she crumpled to the floor. It wouldn't have been so bad if the same thing had not happened to her before. Dad was concerned, so they made an appointment with the doctor. The next week she was in doing all the standard tests and all they had left to do was to wait.

The phone call came not that long after, and it was conclusive that she had Cervical Cancer. The doctor explained that it was a pretty common procedure to go in and scrape the cancerous cells off the cervix. A round of radiation therapy was also recommended. He said this was usually successful with little chance of reoccurrence.

The procedure went well, the doctor was very satisfied with the outcome and mom went home to recuperate. Unfortunately, a few months later, the fainting and nausea returned. The doctor checked and was surprised to see the growth of cancer cells in her cervix again. He ordered more tests; ones where she would have to go off Island. This scared the young couple who had no idea what it all meant.

At the specialist clinic in New Brunswick, my parents sat outside the doctor's office waiting and hoping that it was not serious. Soon they were called in and asked to sit down. The doctor looked at the file a few minutes before he looked up at the young couple. Clearing his throat, he looked at my young mother and said, *"Mrs. Pellissier, I regret to inform you that you have Lymphatic Cancer. Do you know what that means?"*

What it meant, the doctor told them, was that she had a year, maybe two, to live. He also explained that she would be very, very sick for the last little bit of her illness. Their romantic dream was over.

Tears spilled from her eyes as she thought of leaving this man she loved and her two-year-old baby girl. My father looked at his beautiful twenty-three-year-old wife and felt totally help-less. How could he fight this disease? It wasn't a drunken father-in-law or an angry brother-in—law. It was as if death grabbed hold of her and there was no way he could save her.

Over the next year and a half, the young couple tried radiation and chemotherapy; and they both prayed a lot to heaven to spare her life. The sickness soon took hold and my very sad mother said goodbye to the beautiful green house she loved, and into the hospital she went for her last stay.

Dad and I visiting mom at the hospital

She Was Just So Sick

Who would have thought this beautiful twenty-four-year-old Indian princess would have it all taken away in less than two years. With all the treatments, her face was all bloated and her hair had all fallen out. The lymph nodes in her neck and groin were painfully swollen and red. She would cry for pain medication hours before she was allowed more.

Dad would try and be strong when he would come in, but I would look with horror at this creature who was once my mother. It was terrifying what disease could do to the body, still leaving the mind sharp enough to feel each shot of pain and see each sad nod of the doctors and interns who came to see her. Time was running out for her and she was devastated that her prayers were not being answered for the sake of her husband and her child.

The pain became so great they soon gave her a permanent epidural so she would no longer feel anything below her waist. She still moaned with the pain in her neck and under her arms as each lymph node became swollen with tumors. Thoughts of what her life could have been without this illness came less and less as she fought every minute to keep some dignity.

Things were not going so good for dad either at this time. Having a young girl to look after and having a job that made him have to travel all around the Maritimes made his life very difficult. Finding time to see Maggie was getting harder and harder, and the emotional toil was adding up too. There were times when he would just sit and cry and wonder if things could get any worse. Loneliness was a constant companion, with his family so far away and very few friends around who could help him through this. It all seemed so bleak.

His heart was slowly breaking and his best friend was in a hospital. Instead of being able to help him, she needed him to be strong for her. Death is scary for the elderly who have lived their lives and slowly come to grips with leaving the mortal coil. For a twenty-four-year-old, death is a horrifying figure stealing a person away from all she holds dear.

It was at this time that dad was told that he was missing too much time. Red was all my dad could see as his eyes narrowed and he took a big deep breath between his grinding teeth.

"My wife is dying and there is no choice about my priorities. They are with her. Do what you want with that." There, he'd said it out loud. She was dying. His anger left the second he slammed the door. He went straight to the hospital.

A couple of days later, my dad went in to see my poor mother. She seemed a little better. She smiled and said she'd had the most amazing dream. She was in this bright beautiful place and she was surrounded by all these beautiful women who were brushing her hair and talking to her in some unknown language. She felt such peace there. Their hands were taking away the pain that wrecked her body and their brushes were making her hair grow down to her waist again. Dad cried on the way home, wondering if it this dream was a sign or just another cruel delusion of a sick body looking for some peace. It made him wonder.

The Night She Died

Dad was told that his job the next day was to leave the Island to deliver some cheques in New Brunswick so he phoned the hospital to see how his wife was doing. The nurse said that today was not a good day and he should come in. As fate would have it, he thought he would be able to go and do what he had to and he would visit her once he was done. That day though, things did not go as planned. People did not show up as scheduled and other things were delayed. It was quite late when he finally reached the Island, so he decided he would go in first thing the next morning to see my mom.

Early that next morning the phone rang at the green house and someone said, *"I'm sorry to inform you, Mr. Pellissier, your wife has just passed away."*

Many miles away down in Charlton, Eleanor and Carroll were woken from their sleep by a pounding on their guest bedroom window; the very room where my mom had slept a few years earlier. A beautiful bright red cardinal was thrusting his body painfully against the fragile window pane. The old couple watched the bird slowly get up and fly off into the night. Shivers ran through both of them but no words were said as they climbed back into bed. Neither one of them were surprised when their son phoned later that day to let them know his beautiful wife had passed away. They quietly looked at each other and thought of that bright red vision of death that had broken their sleep the night before. My father was numb.

At twenty-nine he had lost the love of his life. Mom's family wept and clung to each other for support when they heard the news. They had lost their beautiful little sister. How could the world ever be right again?

Cross donated in Margaret's memory

The Grave and the Cross

The funeral was planned and dad bought a family plot at the local cemetery. Everything was ready. First, they had a wake on Lennox Island. It was like a bad dream to see this beautiful young woman lying so quietly and still in the coffin. Family members shuffled by and wept as they looked at her beautiful face. A few mourners insisted on taking pictures of my mom all peaceful in death, but that wasn't discovered till much later.

The day that my Mom was buried in the cold ground, covered with dirt, with the stone laid to rest on top, was a sad one. The stone read "Margaret Mary Pellissier, Wife of Louis Pellissier". It stood in the far corner of the cemetery and looked so alone and so sad. The long grass surrounding the cemetery moved with the motion of the wind as family and friends quietly said their goodbyes.

It is very sketchy here for me, but I do remember crying because my daddy was crying and that hurt me inside. It scared me to see him cry. This must be bad. Graveyards must be places where mommies go who never come back.

Granny and grandpa donated a large wooden cross in memory of their Maggie. It hangs inside the front of that little church on Lady Slipper Drive, right where the whole congregation can see it each and every Sunday. On the little gold plaque at the bottom of the cross it says, "Dedicated in Memory to Margaret Pellissier." No other words were needed to express the loss of one so loved and so needed.

The Slap

The spiral effect started soon after the funeral. My dad was called into work a few short days later and told that his position was changing over, and he was no longer needed. Now he had to look for a job, look after a three-year-old and keep up his new house. The stress was overwhelming.

A few days after this, dad went out to get the mail while I played upstairs. When he came back the door was locked, so he started to bang on the door. I was so busy upstairs that the banging meant nothing to me; I just continued to play. Dad ran to the other door that was also locked, so he went back to the front door where he could see his keys on the kitchen table. This just made his temper snap. All his anger and misery flowed out to that locked door. He kicked and punched that door till finally the window shattered.

This noise got my attention and I came running down into the kitchen just as he was reaching in to unlock the door through the broken window. Looking at the keys and me, he walked up and slapped me. The shock of this act made me numb. Only a few loose tears fell down my cheeks as I stared at him. Anger and pain instantly disappeared into shame at the look in my eyes. He fell to his knees and held me close till we both stopped crying.

It was forgotten by the end of the hug for me, knowing that everything was all right again, but for dad, it was a different story. It really made him think.

Going to Grandma's for Awhile

That night dad thought and thought. He knew he needed time to get his life back together, so there was only one thing for him to do and that was to send me to Charlton for a little while. That would give him the time to find a job and become a little more stable emotionally.

I got my ticket, and had all the stuff I would need for a few months, and away I went to Charlton. It is all a little vague in my memory. All I remember is that grandma enrolled me in the nursery program at the local school. It was fun, I remember, listening to all these friends who had the Massachusetts accents. They all thought I spoke funny.

It must have been near the end of the school year because before too long we had our nursery grad party. Grandpa took me into Worcester to buy a pretty dress for the big day. That is where we got to go in the middle of the football field on a stage and sing 'I'm a Yankee Doodle Dandy', and of course, the American national anthem. Granny and grandpa were very proud of me up on that stage. Then I was on my way back home to my dad.

Part Two

The
Green House
Grand River

Ta'pu

Our Beautiful Green House

Coming back home was like jumping into a nice warm bath. It made me feel warm and happy just driving up the little driveway to our green house.

A brief explanation of our perfect house would be that my bedroom was upstairs by the bathroom and dad's room was downstairs in between the family room with our coal stove and our kitchen. Then we had, like, an old dug out cellar we had to access from outside. Off the kitchen was the cutest little pantry with a window that looked over the next door neighbor's fields. Our kitchen had a big old stove; one of those old ones with a heater oven on the top. There were also two doors, one in the front with the glass panes and one in the back that led to a little porch. The rest of the house I did not spend too much time in, so it just appears black in my memories.

The house was located just off Lady Slipper Drive in Grand River and the front windows looked out to the ocean and past all the flowers in our front lawn. It has been torn down since, but still lives strongly in my memory.

This house was so big inside and beautiful. It even smelled of home when you were in there. To get upstairs off the kitchen, there was a narrow dark stairway that curled all the way up to the second floor. There was also an attic but I was never in there. I just knew it was there by the window way up high in the front of the house. Many hours I would stare at that window and wonder what was inside it, but never would I venture there.

The kitchen had a little round table and a light with a million colours that hung from the ceiling. You could spend hours looking at the different colours all over the wall, reflected by that light.

After I came back from Charlton, there was nothing left in the house that would even remind me of my mother. It was just all gone. The bathroom just held a shaver for dad and some deodorant. The bedroom held none of my mother's clothes with her lingering scent. It didn't make me sad at the time. It just made me forget more and more as the days went by. Soon she didn't exist to me anymore. She was just like a woman in a dream. You'd remember her when she was mentioned, but other than that, she stayed in your dreams.

The big green house

Why Protestant?

My Mom was Catholic. Everyone in her family was Catholic. When she was sick in the hospital, the local priest would come and tell her if she prayed hard enough she could be cured of this disease, so every day she would pray as hard as she could. She was never ready to accept dying and that made it hard on everyone. Coming to terms with death is part of the process. Dad felt that the church had interfered with her dying process and it hurt him greatly.

After this, we went to a Protestant church; and mom had a Protestant funeral and was laid to rest in a Protestant cemetery. This decision changed how our lives would go from the moment my dad changed faith for us.

We were not Catholic, and that caused another rift between my dad and my mom's family. They were very upset about how the funeral was arranged. From then on out I think that my dad was slowly separated from the Bernard family, not with family love, but belongingness. Religion is, and has always been, a thing that can bring people together but also tear people apart.

The Crows and My First Kiss

Dad was looking for work so he needed to find a place for me to stay while he was away. Just down the street was a family with the last name of Crow. There was a husband who was a farmer. I knew he grew corn, but I'm not sure what else. The wife stayed home with two older girls and a little boy my age. His name was Kent and he had bright red hair and a whole face full of freckles. We became best friends instantly, since he liked picnics and I loved bugs.

A few times I'd come over and Kent's sisters would have their boyfriends over. That meant we had to stay out of the living room because they would snuggle up on the couch real close and be hugging and kissing. Kent and I avoided them when this happened because they would start screaming and yelling at us if they saw us nearby. We'd go outside and look for bugs or go on wild adventures through the cornfield. The only place we were not allowed to go was near the beach. We'd get spanked for sure if we played near the water.

Kent's sisters would bug us when it was just them around. They'd say things like, "Oh Kent. Here comes your girlfriend." Eventually we decided that we must be in a very serious relationship if his sisters were acknowledging it. One afternoon after seeing Kent's sister hugging and kissing her boyfriend on the couch, we went to Kent's room and went into his closet to talk this out. If we were boyfriend and girlfriend, maybe we should start kissing too.

We both squished our eyes closed and moved towards each other and, as soon as our lips touched, we jumped apart like we were shocked. There, now we were official. For the rest of my time with the Crows, Kent and I would walk hand in hand and we just knew it was love. It had to be.

Strangely enough, we kept in touch with each other till I was at least fourteen. Once or twice a year he would send me a letter asking me how I was doing, so if that is not young love, what is?

My boyfriend and I

The Cornfield

There was one day when Kent and I were especially bored and the house was off limits since his mom was cleaning. You just knew that trouble was not too far away for us. Kent's dad came in from the fields and left the great big tractor out in front of the house so he could come in and eat lunch and it looked so neat just sitting there. It was just like a great big Tonka tractor in the sandbox but it was a much bigger toy for Kent and me to play with.

After looking around to see if anyone was around to see us, we climbed up into the great big seat and pretended to play tractor. We were farmers extraordinaire, working the land and bringing in the large crop of corn that was around the house.

There were a lot of buttons and sticks to move around and unfortunately, a key that was left sitting in the ignition. It was like it had a little sign on it that read 'turn me and see what fun will happen'. Before we did this last deed, Kent made the best tractor sound effects while I pressed the pedals on the floor, and he flicked all the buttons on and off and turned the big steering wheel.

This was really fun. Soon we were pretending to drive that tractor to faraway places with dragons and mermaids when all of sudden, Kent turned the key and the tractor started with a loud rumble. Before we knew it, we were headed off the nice safe driveway and right straight for the cornfield that was almost as high as the cab. In my fear, my foot went down hard on the gas pedal. Our tractor went faster and faster. Corn stalks started slapping the cab of the tractor and both of us had tears of fear streaming down our faces.

Kent's dad came running out of the house just in time to see the tractor disappear into the cornfield with two very scared little kids just holding on. He almost choked on his last bite of food that he had forgotten to swallow, so in shock was he. He ran as fast as he could. Soon he climbed up the side of the tractor and slowed the huge monster of a machine down. I think it could have been that my foot was taken off the gas at this point. He finally stopped us and put us on his knees, squeezing us both so tight I didn't think I would catch my breath. Not a word was said in those few minutes. He started backing up through the corn and brought us back to the house. It may have only been a few minutes, but it was a long few minutes of wishing we were anywhere but where we were.

I didn't really know Kent's father but even I could tell he was beyond mad. All the muscles in his neck were sticking out and his cheeks were as red as Kent's hair as we came to a stop in front of the house again.

Once we were stopped, we scrambled off the tractor and Kent was grabbed by the arm and dragged off into the house. Very soon I could hear him crying as he got the spanking of his young life. Soon Kent's dad came out and, with just a glance at me he got back into the tractor and went back to work.

I just sat on the front step and hoped that my dad would come to get me soon so that I wouldn't have to stay around all the angry faces nor see that path the tractor had made through the cornfield. My dad did eventually come to get me, and instead of being all mad he actually hugged me and asked if I was alright. Then and there I knew I was so lucky to have my dad because he cared more about me being alright than wanting to spank me for a stupid mistake. To tell the truth though, although it scared me out of my mind, it did not stop me from being a mischief maker.

A curious mind is a good thing for the growth of a child academically, but it is also a big factor for those children getting in constant trouble. If there is a button, I needed to know what would happen if I pressed it. If there was a pedal, I had to step hard on it; and if there was a tractor sitting in front of me with a key, I had to try driving it.

Me hiding in a tree

Mud Puddles

I'm not sure when it started or even why. Maybe it was because I couldn't go down to the beach by myself. Anyway, I started swimming in mud puddles. On hot spring days I'd strip down to my birthday suit leaving my clothes somewhere safe and dry and jump into the nearest mud puddle and just lay in there for hours. I would get gravel in my hair and ears but it was always bliss for me. All the pictures of me around this time show me swimming in all sorts of different mud puddles.

It could be the deep dark ones around the ditch or the small, shallow ones in our driveway with the warm slimy mud on the bottom. Mud puddles were all the same – warm and comforting. That was the perfect mixture for a mud puddle, and even though the fascination didn't last too long, it really made me happy at the time. It could be I was a water buffalo or an alligator in a past life and the habit was still in there somewhere trying to burst out, or maybe it was just the sweetest sensation to lay in the sun on a warm spring day and wiggle the slimy mud between my toes and my fingers.

Learning to Ride a Bike on a Dirt Road

One day, out of the blue, my dad came home with the prettiest little bike in the world. It was pink and blue and there were streamers coming out of the handles. I was in love with it. There were two little extra tires on the back. Dad said it was to make sure that I didn't fall. It was such freedom going here, going there, all because of my little bike. With those little wheels no one could stop me. I was like a super hero.

Then one day, dad took those cute little training wheels off. That was the end of my world as I knew it. I couldn't ride it without hitting the dirt on our driveway. My legs and elbows were proof of my efforts to conquer this new challenge. Once I leaned the bike against the house and climbed on to see how it felt. Then, of course, I moved the handle bars ever so slowly till me and the bike smashed painfully up against the house. Soon everything hurt and I could not ride my bike anymore.

Everyday after breakfast I would go out and see if I had learned how to ride overnight, and everyday I'd go a little farther and a little farther down that old dirt driveway. By the time all the scabs on my knees had fallen off, I was a pro, and this time, without the baby tires on my bike. I grew so brave I even tried to ride my dad's huge bike in the yard. I learned very fast that I should leave his bike alone.

I was just so proud that I could drive my own bike up and down the dirt lane, around the whole house and even through the grass. I felt that since I learned to do that, I could succeed at anything. I was queen of my own little world.

Clay Bricks and the Oven

With my love of mud puddles, it was only a matter of time that I soon found I also just loved mud. If I wasn't swimming in it, I would be forming wonderful statues that could dry in the sun. It couldn't be that loose gravel and water mud. It had to be that slimy clay that you could make things with or decorate things with like the tree trunks in my yard or the side of our house.

During the summer, one of my favourite things to do to pass the time was to get some old bricks out of the barn and line them up in a spot where the sun could work its magic. I'd fill the inside hollow of each brick with clay and make mud pies. It would usually take a full day in the hot PEI sun but they would dry with the perfect form for me to play house with the next day. Sometimes there would be twenty dried clay bars on our front step just waiting for me to serve them to all my guests who would include a couple of teddy bears and dolls that I would drag outside. Those guests who did not behave were thrown into the rose bush. Etiquette was very important at my tea parties!

One day it was really cloudy and dark outside and I was bored silly. With nothing to do, I stared outside. I could see my mud puddles growing with the rain and I just knew there must be brand new slimy clay at the bottom, so I went outside and grabbed my bricks and filled them up with the gushy clay. Once they were all set out on the front step to dry, I looked up at the cloudy sky and thought they would never dry, so that play became boring too. I went back inside to find something else to do.

Finding something else to do did not take long. I went upstairs to play in one of the spare rooms where I found a little camping oven. It was hidden under a big black cover. As an explorer, I had to see what was hidden in every corner of the house.

Once I had my new treasure uncovered I saw that it had two elements on the top and it had a little mini-oven in the front with the cutest little door that pulled down like a real oven. There were three knobs on the front with pictures of what elements they controlled. Instead of leaving it alone like a good girl should, I dragged it into the hallway near a plug and plugged it in.

First I turned on one of the top elements, and within a few minutes, it got red hot. I smiled with delight at my own little stove. Then I tried the oven and sure enough, the little element in there got all red hot too. At that exact same time I thought of my mud pies on the front step, just laying there with no sun to cook them.

It did not take long for me to be running downstairs to go and grab two clay filled bricks from the front step and bring them upstairs. Two bricks could fit at one time into that little space. After they were in and the little oven door was closed, I turned the knob to as hot as it could go, and I waited. After about ten minutes of checking those mud pies, I started getting bored with my new game. I thought maybe I could get my dinner party all together while my mud pies cooked, and that is just what I did. I left that little oven to cook those pies for me on the hottest setting there was.

About a half an hour later my father came in to the house and started sniffing the rancid air. He went from room to room till he went upstairs and saw the smoke spilling out of the little oven in the hallway. He came running down the stairs carrying that little oven in his arms, a cloud of black smoke streaming out behind him. Then he started yelling, *"Julie, get over here right now."*

I couldn't even think of what he could be mad about. I'd been just playing with my dolls and being just as good as could be. What could I have done? As I was getting a spanking, I was told that dad prevented a fire in our little green house and that those bricks were ready to explode in my little oven. We then talked about things I was allowed to play with and things I should leave alone. A couple of times I wanted to ask if my mud pies were actually done, but I knew that it might not be the best time to ask.

The lesson I learned in this was not to put bricks into any oven, even if it was little, and always to let the sun cook the mud pies; and if I ever did use that oven again, I was to use it outside just to be safe. I continued to play with it, but I never plugged it in again.

Chapter 23

The Sandhills and Ruddy the Fox

The Sandhills is a little island off Lennox Island. Half the Island was beautiful sand dunes and miles of beach. The other half was berry patches like cranberry and blueberry. It took about twenty minutes to a half an hour to go by boat to the Sandhills from the docks at Lennox Island.

I'm not sure who the person was who showed dad the Sandhills for the first time but it was love at first sight. The quiet solitude of his own little island was a very attractive idea for dad. Soon whenever we had some free time, we'd load the tent and some supplies and jump into our little dory, set up our little motor, connect our big fuel tank and head over. The whole boat smelled like gas and fish during this process. Those were the smells that I would get to know well over the next few years; smells that let me know we were taking some holidays.

Many of our trips to the Sandhills were uneventful, but a few times the ocean showed her power over us during the trip. Sometimes I would sit in the front of the boat covered in whatever I could find on board and when I looked up, I could see the waves that looked five miles high ready to wash over us. Then I would look at dad at the back of the boat and his eyes would never waver from the distant little island. During those times I thought we would never make it. I thought we were destined to sink to the bottom of the ocean and that scared me. I would snuggle deeper and deeper into the safety of my hideout and wait till I was told we were there.

Once we got there it was pure bliss. The sun would come out even on a rainy day. We would set up camp, and start to explore. Those days were wonderful, but the nights were even better. Our campfire would keep us warm and amuse me for hours, especially when there were marshmallows. Once the fire died down, the stories would start.

On one of our first visits to the island we saw a little red fox running up over the dunes that looked at us with some annoyance and fear. Dad told me his name would be Ruddy the Fox, and at night I would hear the best stories of Ruddy, his friends and their adventures across the Sandhills.

Ruddy had many animals for friends and he could talk and learn amazing lessons. Once he stole things from the other animals and they got very mad at him. One thing for sure was he was a very clever fox. When he was very young he had a curly tail like a pig and he lost it. He tricked and tricked all his friends till finally he got a long beautiful tail to match his bright red coat. The stories of Ruddy would wind their way into my dreams and the stories would come to life before my sleeping eyes. For many, many, years I thought that Ruddy the Fox could talk and trick all his friends with his cleverness once the sun went down.

The saddest time was when the tent came down and the ashes from the fire were spread around. Dad always felt he should leave it as he found it, untouched and beautiful. Then we would trek across the dunes and through the berry bushes and back to the little boat. If I was lucky, the ocean would be calm as glass, and the trip across would be a real treat. Then back to the real world where dad had to work long, hard hours, and I would miss being around him so much.

My German Shepherd, Ravey

The first pet I remember having was Ravey, our beautiful German Shepherd. Dad would say he was my protector and best friend. If I wandered far from the house, I could climb on top of him and he would take me home.

Once dad's boss stopped by and I was sitting by myself in the front yard. He walked over to say hi and before I could answer, Ravey was there snapping and growling and he chased the poor man all the way back to his car. Once his door was closed, my loyal friend came over to where I was sitting and lay down next to me to make sure I was okay.

After only a few months, my beautiful dog was shot by a neighbor who thought he was a coyote looking to eat his chickens. Without my best friend around, even the green house lost some of its magic.

The Washing Machine

In the pantry of our house was a machine. It was a huge scary loud machine that I hated from the first moment I remember seeing it. It had a big white tub in the bottom with an arm inside that grabbed the clothes and whirled them around the tub. That was not the scary part though. The two big rollers on the top were the scary part. Their only function was to squeeze the water out of the clothes. The rollers grabbed the clothes from my dad's hands and pulled them through. During this process, water would be coming out of the rollers and if the clothes were too big, those rollers would start to squeal.

Once when I was feeling brave, I offered to help with this big job but I was told I might get my fingers pinched. This thought scared me more than the sounds this horrible machine would make. I then and there became the washing machine patrol. I would watch very carefully to make sure that machine would not grab my father and roll him through. As much as I hated that machine, I loved my dad more, and wanted to make sure he was safe. I would grab a chair and watch till he was ready to hang the clothes on the line. This was my job, protecting my dad from the washing machine monster, and I took this responsibility very seriously.

The Nightmares Begin

When you are little and have a bad dream, you wake up, and with a hug, the nightmare just fades away. When this nightmare comes back time and time again, you remember it your whole life. It returns in times of stress.

The nightmare started out with me looking for my dad. I could hear him upstairs. I started up the stairs behind the kitchen that wound around the wall to the second floor. Once I got near the top, I could hear him downstairs, so I looked through the railing, and I fell. As I fell, I felt like a leaf, swaying this way and that, until I hit the floor and cracked into a million pieces. When I awoke, I had a scream stuck in my throat that came out as a wheeze. I tried not to go back to sleep, but every time I closed my eyes and fell asleep that same dream came again.

As I got a little older, it changed a little where I would see a ladder leading up to the attic window and I'd climb up. As soon as I would start to see what was inside, a pair of hands would come out of nowhere. There was no body, just hands, and they pushed the ladder away from the house; and I started falling again, straight to the ground.

This led me to hate that attic. The only thing that helped me through was that my dad was there every time I woke up from a nightmare. His soft voice and big bear hugs would make it all better. He would put all those shattered pieces of me back together again every night.

The Barn and the Rats

Behind our little green house was an old barn. In my mind, it had been there since the dinosaurs. The sides were full of old rotting hay, maybe put there years ago to feed hungry animals like cows or horses, but left to rot when the farmer sold the place. The great thing that was there was a rope swing. It hung from the centre of the barn and if you ran with it and hung on you could swing so high it felt like you could touch the roof. It was hours of entertainment for me there. I could swing slow and close my eyes, or go real fast and spin round and round.

The only time I could not play in the barn was the spring. Once the snow all disappeared from the yard and the spring sun started to wake up the trees, we had company from that little barn. Once a year, like clockwork, you could look outside and see three or four lines of rats walking from that old barn towards the house.

We knew they were coming because the hay would come alive with little wiggling bodies that were all hungry. Once they got to the house you could hear the walls come alive with the sounds of rustling and squeaks. You could hear where they were and every year we would fight them off with traps, poison, brooms or whatever else we had available. Since we were used to this, it became like finding an ant in your kitchen. We were annoyed but it was not a big deal. The price of living in our big green house was sharing it with about a hundred little guests once a year. To us it was worth it.

Sink or Swim with the Sharks

Like most kids on Lennox Island, we learned to swim the hard way. It was called the sink or swim method of teaching the kids how to swim. If you were near the wharf in the summer, you were a prime candidate for swimming lessons, Lennox style. You were thrown in with your clothes and shoes on and had to make it back to the ladder to get out of the water. The upside of this was you learned how to swim.

I'm sure it was to protect me and keep me away from the water that my dad told me that there were sharks in the water around PEI. The fact that he said sand sharks meant nothing to me. All I heard was the word shark and I was terrified I'd be eaten in one bite if I went near the water.

Sand sharks do live around PEI but they are the size of a large trout and have never, to my knowledge, eaten a little girl for supper; so, the day I unwittingly walked out onto the wharf during swimming lessons time, I almost lost my mind. Into the water I went, and all I could think about was a huge shark coming up to eat me. I think I learned how to swim very, very fast. I almost flew to the ladder and up onto the wharf. It must have been quite the sight to see this young girl trying to count fingers and toes as she ran back to her grandma's house to make sure no part of her had been eaten.

Chickens Still Run When Their Heads are Cut off

Once when I went over to visit friends up the road from us, I was invited to help with chopping day. I didn't really understand what it was or what I had to do so I stood back to see what the other kids were doing first. The kids were all gathered around to catch the loose chickens in the yard and I thought it would be fun to be a part of this game. The chickens were faster than I thought. Even though they ran with a wobble, they were still very hard to catch.

In the middle of the yard there was a great big stump and my friend's mom stood by it with an axe. Nothing connected for me till one of us caught the first chicken. He brought his trophy over to his mom and with a few finely tuned strokes, she had that chicken on the cutting block and BOOM, the head went flying off. What was even stranger was once she let that chicken loose, the headless chicken ran into the tall grass leaving a trail of blood as it ran, I thought, to get away. The game stopped being fun as I felt my lunch slowly coming back into my throat.

The kids went running into the grass to find and bring back the twitching body of that lifeless bird and it went into the dirt by the stump. Their mom asked if I would help pluck the feathers off if I did not want to chase the chickens anymore. I looked at the blood soaked body still slightly twitching in the dirt, shook my head 'no' and ran home to find my dad so I could ask if what I saw was allowed.

Potato Fields Meant Supper

Times were tough after my mom passed away; not that we were rich before, it just seemed even harder to make ends meet after. One thing we did learn is that if you live by a potato field, you will never go hungry. We could have potato soup, potato pancakes, potatoes cooked with corned beef hash or potatoes mashed, deep fried, baked or boiled. The thing that changed was what you had with your potato.

During the hard times, it would be a can of corn deep fried in the frying pan with potato cubes, and a can of sardines on the side. This was our staple when times were tough. During good times we would have potato mixed with a can of salmon and baked in the oven with cheese. We did not eat like kings but we were also never hungry with the potato field beside us. Many years later, there is still no meal for me that does not include potatoes, besides maybe pizza.

Christmas

Now, like most kids, Christmas was a special time, made more so by the thoughts of Santa and his elves making toys all winter. At our house, we had to choose one special gift at Christmas that you really, really had to have, and you made sure to ask Santa for it. You always had to put a lot of thought into this gift because once you wrote it down, that was it.

One thing I learned when I was little was you also had to be specific. If you asked for just a doll, you could get any doll. If there was something you really wanted, you had to be very careful when you wrote your Santa letter.

Christmas Eve was a time when dad and I would sing Christmas carols and spend time looking at our tree, if we were not at my grandparents' house. Our tree had to be a real tree so that the smell would travel through the house, and when you woke up every day, you knew Christmas was coming.

Christmas day always started with breakfast, which was the hardest meal to eat as you could see the presents under the tree and the full stockings around the fire place. Once we had eaten, it was time. We got our stockings and inside were always the yummiest treats. Near the top were great big navel oranges, bigger then my hands, and so juicy, and at the bottom was Christmas ribbon candy. That is the candy that has three or four flavours all wrapped into one ribbon of yummy goodness.

Then it was time for the presents. First would be the present that you asked for, and then you would get the other presents that were mostly things I needed like socks and clothes and some girly things like hair clips or if I was lucky, a pretty purse. Christmas was always special and had this magical feeling like this was the day something extra special could happen.

My favourite gift, when I was little, was a little piano. It only had about twenty keys and most of them sounded alike but it was mine, and I loved it. I was Mozart that Christmas morning; a young protégé who could someday conquer the world. My three children have had a chance to play with this little piano growing up and I can see in their eyes that they can see their potential grow with this simple gift. The little musical book has been gone for a number of years now, yet my little piano still holds the same magic it did on Christmas day many years ago.

The Babysitter and Our Coal Stove

One night in the middle of winter, my dad had to go out, so he got a young girl from up the road to come and watch me. She liked playing dolls so it was okay with me that she came over to play.

Shortly after my dad left, she got a little cold. I told her that what we did when it got cold was we added coal to our little stove and it heated up the house, so she shovelled some coal into that stove. We waited a minute or two and she was still cold, so we shovelled in some more. Soon we had that little stove filled to the top with coal. We could not put one more piece in so we stopped.

Very soon we were playing in another room and the house got warmer and warmer. We were taking our sweaters off and actually starting to sweat from the heat. Dad came home just around that time, and looked at our red faces from the heat, and in two winks of an eye he ran to the stove that was sitting there as red as fire in our living room. He grabbed the shovel and started to shovel the red hot coal from that little stove out into the snow. Soon the house started to cool down and our bright red stove returned to its usual black colour.

I don't think we ever had that girl come back again. Come to think about it, I don't think dad went away in the evening for a very long time after that either.

Don't Answer the Phone
When You're in the Tub

One day when I was away, my father decided to have a bath upstairs. As soon as he got all settled, the phone rang. Usually he would let it ring but he was expecting an important call, so up he got to grab a towel and make the run to the phone downstairs. The first stair was fine, but with wet feet, the second step caught him, and he flew down those winding stairs till he slammed his arm into the wall to stop his fall.

As he lay at the bottom of the stairs, every inch of him that had hit the steps as he went down, was on fire; and, the phone stopped ringing. Trying to answer that phone cost him a couple of broken ribs and a broken wall. When I got home, he was all wrapped up with bandages around his chest, and that hole in the wall just screamed out the danger of those stairs again to me. I don't think either one of us remember who was calling. We just remember the days and weeks it took for him to heal after his fall.

The Clam Ate My Tooth

When the weather was warm, our neighbors would come over and we would spend the day on the beach digging clams. When we had a full bucket we would all go back to the house and set the big pot on the stove. Once the clams were cleaned and the water was boiling, it was time to start cooking. While waiting, we warmed up the butter and had a few dishes set up on the table, all ready for the feast.

One particular clam bake night, I had a loose tooth, my very first one. We had built up the day that it would fall out and I would put it under my pillow to see what the tooth fairy would bring me. I was so excited that soon I would get my first tooth fairy money, which I heard was pretty good; maybe even a whole quarter. The candy I would buy with that made me so happy, but back to the clam bake.

Soon the clams were ready and the water was drained. The pot was set in the middle of the table for everyone to dig in. The shells were cracked apart just enough for us to reach in with a fork and grab out the yummy meat and dip it in the warm butter and swallow it whole with maybe one or two chews.

After a few clams went into my tummy, I felt something strange in my mouth; a hole where my loose tooth had been. I started screaming and holding my belly. Everyone ran over to see what had hurt me and all I could do was cry and hold my belly.

In between loud sobs, I finally got out, " *The clam, he ate my tooth dad.* "

Everyone started laughing which made me screech even louder. How would the tooth fairy find my tooth in the clam inside my stomach? I don't think I have ever had a taste for clams since. The tooth fairy came that night and left two quarters under my belly where that tooth lay.

Driving across the Ice and the Ferry

Before the causeway was built connecting Lennox Island to the mainland, getting across the ice in the winter was always tricky. During the summer there was a ferry that took the cars across, but in the winter the cars had to drive across that ice. In the middle of winter there were rarely any accidents when driving across, but when spring was coming and black ice grew, getting across could be a scary thing.

Dad would tell me when I was a baby and he would go across the ice in the tricky season, what he and my mom would do is drive across with the doors open and me in her lap. The reason being was that if they heard the ice start to crack they would have an easier time getting out and letting the car go down, and if they still had time, at least they could throw me on the ice for someone to find. Their thoughts were at least I would survive if the car went down.

I do not remember that, but I do remember the ferry to and from PEI. You would drive on and see PEI just in the distance. Once the ferry started, the loudspeaker would always play the old song, 'Farewell to Nova Scotia'. Dad and I would always sing it as we left the mainland and looked at our home coming closer and closer.

Sleepwalking and Dad's Fright

We went to visit some friends in Montreal for the weekend. It was an adventure. We drove and drove from PEI. When we got there, we brought in our overnight bags and got all settled in and I fell asleep. Dad tucked me in and went to visit his friends.

He was so happy to be visiting these friends, he stayed up later then he expected. On his way back to his room, he decided to check on me. He looked in my room and I was not there. He checked the bathroom, his room, the kitchen, everywhere, and there was no Julie. He started to panic and think maybe I had gone outside in the middle of this huge city. I would be hard to find if I was lost, so he sat on the couch clearing his head and he thought. If I was in my room at home, where would I walk to climb in bed with him? He ran to the room I had been in and retraced the steps to where his room would be at home. It took him to the porch, and sure enough there I was curled up by the back door sleeping on the floor. I had sleepwalked to where I thought my dad was. He carried me to his room and tucked me in next to him. There was no way I was getting out of his sight for the rest of our visit.

In the morning I had no idea what everyone was talking about. It was a mystery to me. Sleeping in the porch? I could not remember a thing about it.

Last Pee in Bed

This night was so humiliating that it is burned into my memory forever. It started out as a normal night with a glass of juice and water before bed, and then I did what I shouldn't. I fell asleep before I went to go pee for the night.

All night long, I was tossing and turning. My bladder was getting fuller and fuller and the worst thing happened. I dreamed of a bathroom. I ran in, sat down and started to pee. My bladder started to feel so much better but at the same time, a warmth slowly spread all over the bed, and then it got cool. I woke up wondering what had happened. Then I remembered the bathroom in my dream and I started to cry.

Dad heard me crying and came in to see me, so ashamed and confused, and then he saw the bed. He told me it was alright, accidents happen, and we stripped the bed and I got new PJs and, I got to sleep with dad.

The next day I knew it was my fault that we had to fight the washing machine monster, and I watched extra carefully to make sure that no one got hurt over my accident. Once the sheets were safely hanging on the line, I started to feel a little better, but I knew I would never allow myself to dream of bathrooms in bed again.

Daycare for a Day

When dad got a new job, it was time to find someone to watch me, and the first place was the local daycare. I was all excited and waited for my first day. When I got there, I looked at all the toys and all the kids and got so excited. This would be my new place.

By snack time, I was the boss. I took the trays around to give snacks to the other kids and helped feed the babies at the centre. Lunchtime was the same. I went to the kitchen to help out and do as much as I could there. After lunch, we had nap time. Instead of sleeping, I helped rub the backs of the kids who had a hard time sleeping and soon it was time to go home.

After telling dad everything I had done that day, he got upset. He did not send me to daycare to be a worker there. He wanted someone there to look after me, so, my first day of daycare was my last day of daycare. I went back to the Crows the next day. I was there till we left PEI.

What is a Draft Dodger?

The first few times I went to see my grandma and grandpa, I had to go by myself. They lived in Charlton Massachusetts, so sometimes they would drive to pick me up, and once in awhile, I would fly down to Boston where they would come and get me.

I never understood why my dad could not come with me. It was like, if I wanted to go there, it was always by myself. After one of my visits, I finally got dad to tell me about it. He explained that he was a draft dodger. He did not want to fight in the war so he took the Underground Railroad to Canada. He ended up in Quebec where he finished his university. His very first job was on Lennox Island. Since he would not fight for the country, they would not let him back in. He said that the war that they wanted him to fight in was not right and he could not support it, so he left. It was a few years later that the administration changed and Jimmy Carter changed that law. Everyone was allowed back into their country.

We only visited there. It was not somewhere we wanted to live, but it was great that I could go to visit my grandma and grandpa with him! They missed their baby boy so much.

Part Three

Charlton,
Massachusetts

Si'st

Granny and Grandpa

My granny was a young beautiful English girl when she met my grandfather, a young French man. She felt bad for him the minute he introduced himself as Carol Pellissier though; not only was his first name a girl's but his last name was French, and in New England in the early 1900s, being French was not that popular.

They soon fell in love and were married. They had their first son and my granny wanted more. After many years, they gave up and adopted a young girl from an orphanage. Once they got her home and set up, sure enough, granny found out she was pregnant. Fifteen years after her son was born, her second son, my father, was born.

My grandpa was a writer. He wrote for different magazines and newspapers over his career. I had a special bond with both of them. Grandpa spoiled me. I was always treated like a little princess when I was there. Granny was amazing at telling stories of when she was young, and I loved to sit for hours listening to her.

Granny collected things and sold them at the Flea Market, so her house was always a treasure trove of fascinating objects, from bottles to buttons and crafts from all over. Grandpa was a little bit old school. Suppertime was always an event. All the food was placed in front of him and he served everyone. You had to be careful how much you asked for because as a child you had to finish your plate or wait hours at the table till you were allowed to leave. Things were as they were there, and once you learned the rules, you were fine.

Aunt Ginny and her Brood

Aunt Ginny had had a hard life. She was adopted as a young girl, she had a bad marriage and one of her children had special needs that required a lot of her time. I did not know what to make of her, except to know she did not get along with my dad for long periods of time. She was a large woman who always seemed cranky so I did not bond with her at all when I was little. I was actually a little afraid of her.

One of her daughters became my friend, but it was a strange friendship. It only lasted as long as I was there. We never kept in contact in between visits. Aunt Ginny had five children and only one of them would be someone who spent time with me when I was little which is strange because they just lived up the road.

The Toy Drawer and the Candy Cupboard

When driving to see granny and grandpa, what I always remember the most is the toy drawer and the candy cupboard. The toy drawer had lots of learning toys that were all so neat. My favourite toy was this wooden lady. When you untwisted her and pulled her apart, there was an exact twin inside, just a little smaller. It was the same with the little one inside there till finally there was a little wee wooden lady. This toy, I could play with all day.

The other place I looked forward to was the candy cupboard. It was way up high and latched shut, so it was definitely a place you had to be invited. Inside were chocolate bars, candy of all kinds and cartons of malted milk balls that were my favourite. If I finished all my supper or helped with cleaning or asked at just the right time, I got an invite to pick something out of the candy cupboard and that was when I knew I was so very lucky.

The Blue Willow China and Aluminum Cups

The table in the dining room at my granny's was made of deep dark wood and it held about nine people in one sitting. Off to the side was a dark wooden cabinet that was not only a treasure in itself, it also held the treasures of the family.

On one side there was a complete set of the most beautiful plates. The design had two little birds facing each other in the top centre, and around them was a Chinese town by water. The beauty and harmony in that picture always made me happy. On the other side of the cabinet were her cups and glasses. They were the same ones that have been there forever; maybe since that cabinet was put in the house.

The family took turns buying granny new glasses each year. She would take them with a smile and a thank you, and then put them down in the cellar with all the other new boxes of special glasses.

The cups were made of metal and came in red, blue, yellow and green. The tops were worn with the years of use and the insides were down to the metal again with all the washes. My favourite was red, so breakfast was not complete without my little red metal cup and blue willow bowl filled with cereal or fruit. I would sit at the table and the sun would sneak in and dance on my red metal cup, and then all over the walls of that little dining room would be dancing red splashes of light.

Bitter Red Mouthwash

The bathroom at my granny's was always filled with little wonders, as was the rest of the house. It had two doors going in; one from the kitchen and one from my room. On the tub was always anti dandruff shampoo, and on the sink was a bottle of red mouthwash.

Every night I would see grandpa brush his teeth and then swish this red mouthwash around his mouth. It didn't look so bad, so one day I decided to try it. As soon as it touched my lips I could feel the burning and heat from this red, bitter mouthwash. For a split second I thought for sure, I had lost all the skin from the inside of my mouth. Tears were streaming down my face as I spit it out into the sink.

It was not the experience I thought it would be, so I told my cousin, who would visit with me there. We soon made a competition of who could keep that burning liquid in our mouths the longest. The bottle said cinnamon mouthwash. I was sure it was poison. I don't think I ever won that competition, but I kept trying.

Granny's Beautiful Hair

Granny always kept her hair parted on the side and pulled back into a bun at the back of her head. Ever since I could remember, her hair was snow white with little sprinkles of gray. If I got up extra early, I would go to her room and see her at her dressing table brushing out her hair for the day. Her hair went all the way down her back with several waves here and there. As she brushed, if the sun was out, the sun beams would come into her room and her hair would just glitter and shine with each stroke.

I knew this was special because no one saw granny with her hair down, so I would watch quietly until she was done. First, she would do her part on the side and pull it all back into a pony tail, then she'd wrap the hair up around the pony and clip it all in.

She was a fragile beauty, never loud or boastful, also soft spoken, and gentle to hug and even talk to. When I told her how beautiful I thought she was, she would smile and say, *"You're full of hokum."* I was never really sure what that meant, but it made her smile, so I would too.

Some of My Favourite Meals

Besides always having fruit from the orchard around, granny was a good cook. One of my favourite meals was spaghetti goo. Whenever she would cook it, she would say, *"Now this is a meal just for kids; only kids like it. When you get to be all grown up, you will not like it anymore."* I didn't understand. How could anyone not love this meal?

First she would cook half a pot of spaghetti, and when it was done and drained, she would add a can of tomato soup and half a block of Velveeta Cheese, and stir it all up till all the cheese and soup were mixed in, and it was a gooey, steamy pot of yumminess. It was so yummy for a child raised on meat and potatoes. You don't realize food can have that much flavour when your taste buds feel like they are dancing with each bite.

A few others that she would make were corn fritters, frankfurters and beans with homemade molasses bread, and pea soup and johnnycakes. Of all the meals she ever made for us, these ones I still remember and can taste in my mind.

Time Out and What Happened

Suppertime was always something everyone looked forward to. You could smell it start cooking in the afternoon, and just as you couldn't take it anymore, it was time to sit at the table. Everyone would sit down and wait for grandpa to sit and say grace. Once that was done, granny would go back to the kitchen and grab all the food and bring it in and place all of it at the head of the table. Then, one by one, we would pass our plates up to be filled.

Once your plate went up the line, you were asked how much of this you wanted and how much of that you wanted; and what I usually forgot, was to ask for a little, and then ask for seconds. I did this because grandpa was very stern about cleaning your plate. If you asked for too much you were left at the table till you could finish it.

One evening I was so very, very hungry, and we were having my favourite spaghetti goo. I asked for a great big plateful and once I was about half done, I started feeling full. I looked at my plate and waited. Maybe if I waited a little bit, I could finish it. That idea did not work. As soon as grandpa was done, he looked down the table at me and said, *"You can leave the table once you are done."*

So, I sat; I moved the spaghetti this way and that way on the plate; I twirled it around my fork to make little mounds of spaghetti; nothing worked. Now, cold spaghetti goo is not at all the same as hot spaghetti goo, and even with a mouth full of milk, it still did not taste good at all. For me, it seemed like hours just sitting there, looking at that plate, hoping it would get smaller if I looked away long enough, but spaghetti does not shrink over time. Then grandpa came in and said, *"If you can't eat it, then go to your room and stay there for the rest of the night."*

Well, I was furious. I ran to my little room stomping as loudly as I could to scream my discontent without words, and with a loud bang, I slammed the door. Then I sat down and looked around my tiny little prison. There was a bookcase, my little bed and granny's writing desk so the bookcase, which was closest, got it first. Every book got taken out and thrown to the ground. My blankets came off the bed and my pillows went this way and that. After I was done venting my frustration, grandpa walked in and looked around and all he said was, *"You have ten minutes to clean up this mess, little girl."*

Now, even though I was mad, I still knew his temper was worse than mine, so those books were all put back in place and the bed was made nice and neat. By the time he came back, everything was as it was before my tantrum. When he walked back into the room and saw the room was fixed up, instead of still being mad, he sat down and gave me a big hug. Our battle of wills was over and for some reason, I think we both won that night because I was never given more then I could eat at supper, ever again; and grandpa knew my worst, and to him, it wasn't that bad.

My Friend, Mike Stepson

Across the street was an older farm owned by the Stepsons. They were very quiet people but I always liked going over there and exploring the farm. They had a boy who was my age named Mike. He had dirty blond hair and freckles everywhere and a smile that went from ear to ear. He was my Charlton friend. We would explore the barn, clean the stalls, watch the cows get milked and jump off the manure shute.

He always made the summer special when he came around. When we hid in the bush above the well, we could see fairies in the sun beams playing overhead. We could see the goblins in every dark corner of the yard when it was dark.

Our greatest adventures started early in the morning when we would travel though several fields and through many forests till we got to the marsh. There, we would catch little newts and frogs and bring them back in our little buckets. When we were on our trips, we were explorers. We were adventurers of the highest rank. We would conquer the many enemies hiding behind the long winding stone fence that guided us to the marsh, and save all the kingdoms we could create in our heads.

I was lucky at that age. It didn't matter if I was a little princess, a daring knight or even a bloodthirsty pirate. There were never, ever any boundaries to what we could think up. There were never dull days when Mike and I were together. We were true heroes, each and every minute.

The New Calf

Late one evening, there was a loud knock on my door. Grandpa got up and answered it, and after a few minutes he came over and told me Mike wanted me to go over to his house for a few minutes. He had a twinkle in his eyes as he said this so I knew I was in for a great surprise.

After I got my shoes on and ran out the door, Mike was there, waiting with a great big smile. He said one of his cows was getting ready to give birth, and he wanted me to come and see. I'd seen kittens come into the world, so I was very excited about this new adventure.

We raced over to his barn and sure enough, there was a big cow tied to a post and Mike's dad was there stroking her sides. Every once and a while the cow would start to shiver from her neck all the way down to her tail. After a few minutes of watching this all unfold in front of me, Mike's dad started to look a little nervous. The cow was getting more and more bothered by the shock waves of pain racing through her. She started to struggle against the rope and give these noises of pain and confusion. Before I knew it, Mike's dad lifted that cow's tail and put his whole arm inside. This made the cow's eyes go up into her head. This had not happened when I was watching the kittens being born. I just stared at the whole scene in horror. Within seconds though, the arm came out and also a set of legs; and soon there was a brand new calf lying in the hay.

The mama cow was untied and went to licking that calf until it was all clean. I think I adopted that little calf in my mind because everyday I would go over and see how it was doing. It grew so much that summer; almost as much as me.

The Treasures of the House and the Flea Market

Every Friday was a fun day at granny and grandpa's house. This was the day we would get ready for the market Saturday morning flea market. This meant we went through the closets and the old barn and gathered all these treasures. Old bottles of different shapes and colours were my favourite treasures. Imagining all the different things that were in them was part of a game I created. Granny also sold old election memorabilia. The names had all faded, but most of them were large posters with great big red print saying, 'Vote for Me'. She also sold collector stamps and old coins and magazines. These were the things that everyone, even then, was looking for.

There was a lot of money in this business, and my grandparents were quick enough to get into it while they could. By the time we were done, the car would be packed for the morning. We would drive to the flea market and set up at a little table.

Half the fun was looking at all the stuff granny had, and the other half was running around to all the other tables and seeing what everyone else had. People had things from the war; more bottles that held mystery ingredients; and ancient kitchen, household and farm appliances that looked like they were from outer space. If you have ever been to one of these, you can imagine how it would look to a young child. It was like being invited to another planet at times. If I was lucky and had behaved for the week, I always got a little something so I could buy a small trinket or two while I was there.

Captain Kangaroo and Mr. Rogers

At home we only had a thirteen-inch TV that would be brought out once or twice a week. The shows that dad watched did not at all interest me. I think there was a war show and the news that he would watch; nothing that captured my imagination in anyway. At granny and grandpa's there were a lot more stations and some of those stations had children's shows that I could not take my eyes off of; two that come to mind were Captain Kangaroo and Mr. Rogers.

The men in these shows were just like big loveable kids and made me happy just to watch them interacting with the rest of the shows' characters. Their reality was that everything was good, people were all nice, and I am pretty sure, there were no little girls without a mommy there.

I would get lost in these shows. Their dramas were always so small and always resolved in a half hour. This started my love affair with the television, the place where I could go with a click of a button to see everything in life as good and just, even if it was for only a half hour at a time.

The television was set up in the living room, and right in front of it were granny's rag rugs and that is where I would sit and watch, captivated, every Sunday morning. The smell of the dust, dirt and numerous pets was absorbed by the rugs, but those were the smells that reminded me that I was where I should be. I was where I was loved, and life was good.

The Outhouse

From the dining room you could go into the old barn that was attached to the house. There were more spiders and dust in there so it was not one of my favourite places, but it also had the little outhouse. It was a little room at the end of the barn where you could go and do your business if the other bathroom was full.

When you went there, through all the cobwebs, and walked into the outhouse, there were licence plates, nailed from floor to ceiling, all over the walls. If you had to stay out there longer than usual, it was a great place to read all the different plates from all the different states; and some from the same states but with different designs, shapes and colours.

Like other outhouses, there was a toilet seat. If you looked down, you got the smell of years and years of foul smells. My trips there were always just as fast as could be just in case there was a spider down there or worse, wanting to bite my most exposed areas.

Everyone would use this during the day, but never, never at night. The spiders would multiply and there would be different scary noises from all over the barn. The skittering of small bodies on the second floor and the scurrying of outside creatures under the floorboards made it really scary during the day; but at night, it was totally off limits.

Rabbits and Groundhogs

The sight of cats and dogs lead me to a story about my grandparents that still makes me smile. When my grandparents were dating and talking about marriage, one of the stipulations of accepting the marriage offer was that grandpa promise granny that she would always be allowed to own a dog and a cat in their household.

Back then, the head of the house was always the man, so making sure the one thing she always wanted was promised before she said 'I do' was imperative. For her, it was not riches or fame or security or unconditional love till the end of time. What she wanted was pure and simple; the right to always have her pets. They always did have a dog and a cat. When she was a very old woman and grandpa had long since passed, she refused to go into a home because they would not take her pets. She lived out her life at her own home, with her animals.

Now, going back in time, this is a very simple story, but one of the hardest to write for me. My grandparents had a great big dog. He was friendly and loyal and would even sit on command when I asked, but one thing he would also do every night in the summer that would break my heart was hunt.

The house would always be very warm in the evening, so almost every evening we would sit outside and tell stories or just watch the sun go down with quiet thoughts of the day.

Once the sun went down, like clockwork, that dog would wander back into the yard with his treasure held firmly in his teeth and then he would drop it at the feet of my grandpa.

The nights he would bring home groundhogs was not too bad. They were bigger and sometimes messier if he had ripped them open during the trip home. It could be really gross with intestines dangling behind the corpse. The smell of blood went right through the yard when the dog did that and also went right through me. Those nights I could handle, but what I hated were the nights that that dog would bring home bunny rabbits. They would twitch and shiver for hours on the ground in front of my grandpa.

Once a child has seen death, any visual reminder of a creature holding onto life, with all its being, brings back the original trauma. The rabbits would have a panicked look in their eyes as they rolled this way and that. The twitches looked like they hurt as much as the trauma of being chewed up by that big dog. If the rabbit was still in one piece, I would grab a towel from the house and sit and rock that little rabbit until the tremors went away, little realizing that that meant that they were dead.

Once I had to go in for the night, I would leave my rabbits outside and hope and pray that my love and attention had saved them, and they would be my pet in the morning. Unfortunately, every morning, I had my hopes crushed. Their little white bodies would be cold and hard by the time I checked on them.

This would mean that it was funeral time. I would dig a hole under the prettiest tree and hold my funeral for each and every rabbit I tried to save. I would say a prayer over the grave and have a cry over the loss of such a beautiful creature.

Once, when I was older, curiosity took over and I thought maybe they had turned into angels so I decided to dig one up. I was excited and anxious to see my little friend again. What I found instead were bones, with tufts of dirty white fur and clumps of rotten meat. Was this an angel or did I not pray hard enough to get them into heaven?

My heart was broken. Death could never be pretty. Going in the ground did not change you into an angel, and I cried for my little rabbit friends and for my mom, who miles and miles away, had her body lying in the cold dark ground too. There could be nothing good about death. It was not a magical transformation for me anymore. It became very dark and ugly for me. I did not tell anyone about this because I knew I had broken a rule by questioning what the adults had told me and looking at what death really was like; so, it sat in my heart for a very long time, always, just below the surface.

Poison Ivy, Fleas and Bats – Oh My

If anyone has had poison ivy, they will know how awful it is. It grew like grass all over Charlton, so that meant that every summer there would be a week of no sleep and lots and lots of scratching and crying. It would always start with a little rash and it would travel like a red fire from one end of me to the other.

To make matters worse, because of grandma's and grandpa's age, they did not look after their pets as they should. If I got a friendly visit in bed from one of the animals, I also got lots of little visitors who pestered me till I thought I would lose my little mind. Fleas are very small and fast. The small table light made it hard to see where exactly they were hiding. The only way you knew they were there was when they started to bite. Then, when the itchy poison ivy and biting fleas were all I could take, the noises started behind my bed.

When I slept upstairs, there would always be night noises in the walls. They would start out as small scratchy sounds and soon grow into a beehive of noises. There was a large air vent by this room, and this is where the bats of the neighborhood decided to make their home. All I could hear on my side of the wall were noises like a hundred bony fingers scraping and scratching behind my bed, and in my mind, they all wanted to come in and poke at me with their long jagged nails.

On these nights, I would slowly drift off to sleep and dream of growing wings and flying out of that air vent into the night sky. I'd dream of soaring and gliding over trees and streams, and dancing with the moonbeams until my eyes would open; and I'd find myself back in bed, looking into the face of granny's cat or dog who'd brought more little visitors into the bed with me.

Making Rag Rugs with Granny

When there was a blanket or shirt too old to mend, granny would put it in the rag basket. By the end of the winter, that old basket would be full of all different sorts of colours, patterns, shapes and sizes of cloth. Then when all of us grandchildren were over, we'd have rag rug night.

Granny would set up her chair outside by the front door, and her basket of rags would be in front of her. Then she would cut a nip into the cloth, and we all got turns taking that strip and running across the yard with it until it came free. My cheeks would go beet red from the running and laughing we would do on these nights. Then we would run back to granny with the long strips and she would lay them across her lap. We all took turns until all the rags were torn into strips.

Once this was done, granny would take those rag strips and start to braid them into long coils we called rag rope. Before the night was done, she would have her sewing needle out and be sewing those ropes into circles and ovals, and that rope would coil around and around granny's sewing needle. Depending on how pretty the rug was, we would have a new rag rug for the front door, the fireplace or one of the bedrooms hidden away. Some would come out with beautiful strong greens and reds and others would be all brown and yellow.

Every room had a rag rug to decorate the floor, and we grandchildren felt like we were a special part in the making of each of those rag rugs. Sometimes I would look real close to see if I could find one of the rag strips I had pulled off, running down the front yard.

Old Sturbridge Village and my Great, Great Aunt Emma's Couch

One of my favourite places to visit when I was little was Old Sturbridge Village. This would always be an all-day event; one that made my mind run wild with thoughts of how things were a long, long time ago. It was like a living museum, with people dressed in old clothes and doing work like they must have done it years ago. Each house was filled with old things. There was a church, a mill and a store where everyone could buy souvenirs and candy.

The day would begin by getting in the car and driving for what seemed like forever till we pulled into the huge parking lot of the little village. On the very best of visits, it would start with very few cars to walk past to the front gate. That would mean that I would have the place to myself and my imagination.

We would go to each and every house, barn and store, and explore each and every path to see where they went. As I walked down the cobblestone streets, I could see the men in the barn milking cows on little three-legged stools with handmade wooden buckets; women making homemade bread in little ovens hiding in the middle of their fireplaces; and children running and playing with old fashioned toys and chasing farm animals here and there. It was magical, it was exciting and it was a place where I wished I could live everyday.

There was one house that we would spend a little more time in, and the tour of it would start in the little kitchen that was

Old Sturbridge Village and my Great, Great Aunt Emma's Couch

filled with marvelous treasures from years gone by. Once we walked through there, we would get to the place with the biggest treasure of all, the sitting room.

Roped off in a secure area was my Great, Great Aunt Emma's old couch. It soon was the highlight of our trip to see our family's contribution to such a wonderful place. Even though this was the same Aunt Emma that once caned my dad for saying 'damn' at the dinner table, I could envision this pristine lady sipping tea sitting on that beautiful couch that would be forever preserved in this little house.

The rest of the day would be at all the other houses and farms where there were animals I could feed and touch if I felt brave enough. When my feet felt like they were going to fall off, we would reach the store. This place held all the little toys and candy that we could buy before we left.

My absolute favourite was this candy on a stick called Rock Candy. It came in all shapes and flavours and it looked like diamonds all glued together. It was hard and sometimes cut the inside of my mouth because it was so sharp, but the sweet flavour made it worth every nick and scrape and made me smile in absolute delight. For weeks after, I would dream of all the wonderful buildings we walked through and imagine that I was actually part of that time period. What joy, what fun, how simple and carefree! This was the place I thought I belonged.

Cousin Marie and the Visit

My cousin Marie was a teenager when she visited me. She was, and is, the most beautiful woman I can remember when I was little. She had long dark lashes that surrounded her beautiful brown eyes, and every time she smiled they would twinkle. I had seen some pictures in a nature book of deer with their deep liquid brown eyes, and that is what her eyes looked like to me, so beautiful. Her long, dark hair had a natural curl at the end that would bounce when she walked, and there was never one of those beautiful hairs out of place on her head.

Her eyes always lit up when she saw me walk in a room, and I was drawn to her warmth and tenderness. Wherever she sat, I had to sit right next to her. Whatever she ate or drank at supper, I had to eat and drink. Even though I was little, she talked to me and made me feel big and special. She would tell me about my mom and how much she loved her and missed her. She told me she had lived with granny and grandpa too when she was younger, and that she loved them for all they had done for her.

She was very brave. She would laugh when grandpa got mad and even tease him back into a good mood. My cousin, Marie was my family, and she was what I wanted to grow up to be like: beautiful, strong and brave. Little did I know then that all those traits could not rub off on me, no matter how close I sat to her, or even if I ate and drank everything that she did.

From her, I learned there are two different kinds of hugs. There is the polite hug and that is just arms lightly draped around your body and the pat on the back hug, and then there is the hug that once you are in it, you feel loved and treasured. With Marie, I would feel the heat from her neck on my cheeks as she would hug my head with hers, and then I would smell her perfume, a soft gentle smell that reminded me of laying in the grass on a sunny day. Then her arms would wrap around my whole little body till I could almost feel like we were melting into one. Marie was my cousin and my friend and I loved her with my whole little being.

The Promise

Grandpa and I always had a strange relationship for as long as I could remember. He was always a 'tell it as it is' kind of grandpa. Sometimes he could be cruel with his approach.

Once when my aunt was over for supper, grandpa announced at the dinner table, she was not to have any of those farter beans in his house. She was a large woman, and I presumed that meant she would have even larger farts if she were to eat those farter beans. She was used to his teasing so she did not even comment back. One of her eyebrows went up as she looked down at her plate, and that was it.

Another time, when we had been driving a long time, I asked if we could stop so I could go to the bathroom. My grandfather, unlike maybe ninety-nine per cent of all other grandfathers, turned and said to me, "*I am not stopping little girl. If you really need to pee, you can pee here,*" and he cupped his hands in front of me. I told him I really did not have to pee that bad anymore, and that was the end of that.

With all of that, it is almost like he knew when I was having a bad day. A new doll or a new outfit would appear in my room on those days that I needed a lift. There was also never a night when grandpa and I were not cuddled up in his big sitting chair reading stories, so I always knew I was his little princess.

One night, we were sitting outside looking up intently at the stars. Grandpa looked over at me and asked me if I believed in ghosts or spirits. I did, or at least I thought I did. I had never seen one, but many, many a time I could feel people around me that weren't there. Sometimes I could hear things too, like footsteps and long drawn out sighs coming from nowhere, so I knew there were ghosts around. I just didn't have proof. Grandpa said to me, as he looked up to the starry night sky that he would give me proof one day.

"When I die, I promise I will come back to you and show you that the spirits are real. I will give you proof, because I love you." Then he looked at me and said, *"It will be our little secret."*

I smiled back at him, but deep down, I was scared. I didn't want proof of this. I was uncomfortable with the spirits I had around me already. I went to bed that night, scared and sad, and the covers went up over my head as the walls became alive with the sounds of wings and claws scraping and scratching behind my head.

Part Four

Back at the
Green House

N a' n

Cathy, the Hippie and her Daughter

Now it took a long time, but soon dad was going out again; not to work and not to visit with friends. He went out on a date. I did not know this until one day he started getting me ready to go out. He had put my prettiest sundress out on the bed. This was reserved for church or special visits so I was curious.

When we were in the car, dad finally said he was bringing me to meet a lady and her name was Cathy. I still wondered why she was so special she deserved my best sundress, but I knew this would be a fun adventure so I just relaxed and enjoyed the ride there.

Once we pulled into her long driveway I could see her long blond hair blowing in the wind and her sundress flowing this way and that. It was only after I got out of the car that I saw the big milk tub with a tiny version of her peeking over the top to see me. Dad told me this was Cathy and her daughter Cora.

Cora was around two or three with straggles of blond curly hair and big blue eyes that seemed to get bigger whenever she smiled at me. I hung onto my dad's leg. I was around five at this time, and I was not too sure about this woman; nor of her little one either.

Dad said he had to leave for awhile, but he wanted me to stay and get to know his new friend, so I stayed. For the first little while I sat on the grass looking at the driveway for my dad to come back, and then slowly I moved closer to the tub as the little one looked like she was having so much fun splashing and swimming in there. After walking around the tub a few times, I put my hand in and let the cool water glide over it. Well, if it felt that good on my hand, maybe I should try my toes in there. As soon as my socks and shoes were off and I was ready just to test the water, along came Cathy; and she said, *"You can't get your pretty sundress wet. I will take it off so you can jump in."*

Before I had time to say, 'no thank you', that sundress was off and sat folded on her deck. The anger came then as I stood there with just my undies. How dare her! How could she! Who did she think she was! I jumped into the tub and sat, little knowing or feeling if the water was hot or cold. I was humiliated. Her little girl kept swimming over and making cute noises to me with her chubby red cheeks, and I would have nothing of it. I wanted my dad. I wanted to go home. Why did we ever have to come here? Soon Cathy took her little girl out, and with a shake of her head, left me alone to sulk.

Before too long my dad did come, but before I could talk to him, she was there, hugging him and whispering something to him, as she pointed to me in the tub and passed him a towel. Over he came and lifted me out and started to dry me off. I told him I wanted to go home, I didn't like this place, I didn't like this lady and I especially now, did not like that milk tub.

Dad said we were staying for supper and we would go right after, so with my sundress on, and my pruned fingers and toes, I waited on the deck. This supper would take forever. Then I noticed the mud. Mud, mud, mud, I loved mud. Mud made me happy and was a great way to make the time go faster. I soon found a little bucket and had just enough mud for a mud pie. I brought my bucket of mud over to the deck and started digging to shape the pie.

Cora soon came over to see what I was doing. She watched and watched me, and a wicked idea came to my mind. I went into the house where Cathy was busy in the kitchen and with my sweetest smile, I asked very politely for a plate and a spoon. She gave me the biggest smile and said, " *Why sure honey. What are you doing?*"

"*Making mud pies,* "I replied, ever so sweetly. Out I went with my plate and my spoon and I waited. Soon little Cora let her curiosity get the better of her and she came over. On my plate was a beautiful mud pie, and I pretended to eat it with so much pleasure. Cora watched and started to smile.

"*Me too,* "she soon said.

"*Do you want some pie?*" I asked.

"*Oh yes,* "she said with delight, thinking maybe I might share some with her.

So, I got her to sit on the deck like at a real tea party and started to do chew-chew train. As soon as she had the spoon of mud pie in her mouth, Cathy came out. Cora started crying. Cathy started yelling. Mud started dripping out of Cora's mouth and that is when dad came out. Within minutes of 'your daughter, my daughter', the screaming began between them, and it ended with my dad saying, "*Get in the car. We're leaving.*"

I got up off the deck and walked to the car, with only one look back and a little smile because I knew I'd never have to go back there again. We were off. There were no more women in dad's life for a long time after that. I sometimes wonder about the two of them and what became of them and that old milk tub.

Sharing the Old Green House

When I came back from granny's and grandpa's place, things had changed. Our green house was still ours, but we had renters. A woman and her three children were there and they took up most of the house. She had two teenage boys and a little girl my age. It was strange having a playmate actually live with you. I was used to having a lot of time by myself, but where I went, she went.

Her name was Becky and she was a little younger than I was, so I got to be the boss and I liked that. We would take turns on the rope swing in the barn and wander around searching for adventures. The older boys were never around, so we only saw them when it was supper and then they would disappear into their rooms.

It worked out for dad, since now I had someone to watch me while he looked for work, and he also had some help with all the bills. She would cook and clean, and all we had to worry about was our room on the far side of the house. Once and a while, dad would complain that one of the boys was going in and taking stuff, but for the most part we all got along fine.

This woman was not overly friendly. Dad said she had a hard life, so I kept my distance and did what I was told with her. Some people you just knew you did not cross in any way, and she was one of those people.

The Barbed Wire and the Boat

One day when the boys were around we all decided to go for a picnic adventure. Their mom was cleaning and did not want us in the house for any reason, so we packed up some sandwiches and off into the woods we went.

After walking for what seemed like forever, we came to a marsh. The ground got all spongy and the sounds and smells overpowered us. Then we saw it, a little dory, leaning on its side at the edge of the water. There were even oars attached to the rim on each side. What an adventure We could be pirate adventurers with our own boat. What fun! What joy! The boys put us two girls in the boat and then lifted and pulled that old boat into the water. Once we were afloat, the boys jumped in and away we sailed. For a few brief moments we were sailors extraordinaire. Then we all looked down, at the same time, to see water rushing in through the many cracks and crannies this old boat had all over it.

"Abandon ship," we yelled and jumped into the marshy water. We were fortunate not to have got caught in the seaweed that grew to the top of the water. Somehow we all glided across the water and back to land.

The only thing I lost were my shoes and there was no way I was going back to look for them. We all smelled of rot, and where there was not green goo on us, there was black goo. We all wanted to go home. The boys decided to run, and my friend and I tried to keep up, but even running as fast as we could we still could not keep up with them.

Soon they were a blur in the forest and even their sounds were gone as well. This was when, with bare feet, I walked right on top of a barb of barbed wire. I could feel it pop through my skin and tickle the bone of my heel. I felt the pain as I pulled my heel off the rusty little swords. I fell forward in tears.

"We have to get home," my friend Becky said. *"I will help you walk."*

Together we hobbled back to the old green house. I was brave and I was strong till my dad came out of the house.

"Daddy, help me. I hurt."

Dad took me to the hospital where the doctor had to remove the tips of those rusty barbs from my heel; not only did they hurt going in but they hurt even worse coming out. Then I had to get a needle because of the rust and, all bandaged up, we got to go home. Not once did dad mention how badly I smelled with the swamp water all around me, but I did get into the tub as soon as we were home all safe and sound.

Boys Really are Nasty – All of Them

Once I was all healed up, Becky and I became closer and closer. She was like a sister to me and we shared everything. Soon we could not be separated. At night I would go to her room, so we could whisper and laugh till we fell asleep giggling, until one night when we talked about the secret.

"I have a secret," she told me. *"Do you want to know what it is?"*

"Yes," I whispered back to her with the anticipation of knowing something new and exciting was taking over me.

"Come with me," she whispered, *"and be really, really quiet."*

We snuck out of her room and went up the scary winding stairway at the back of the house behind the kitchen. These stairs never brought anything good to me, but up I went behind her in the dark being as quiet as a mouse.

Soon we were at her oldest brother's bedroom and she went in. As I got to the door, I could see his bed and a small lamp in the corner giving off only enough light to make creepy, scary shadows all over, and then he sat up in the bed, opened the covers, and tapped the empty spot with his hand as if to say without words *"Come over and jump in."* Becky jumped right in giggling and said "Come on in. It's alright," so I got in and lay down as he put the covers over us all.

Under the covers he started tickling us, and then said, *"Shhh, don't be too loud girls."* Then, after a little while, his hand fell between my legs. Thinking it was an accident, I squirmed away, but it followed me as I turned.

"What is this?" he whispered. Suddenly I realized how close he was to me. Becky slipped out of the bed and went to the door.

"Don't you go yet. I need to talk to you," he said.

I looked at Becky one last time as she closed the door and said, *"I have to go."*

"Show me what this is and I will let you go." Slowly, with a fear I'd never felt before, I showed him. He smiled and said, *"You know this is bad, very bad, and I will tell what you are doing if you don't come back tomorrow."*

Bad? My fault? My dad will think I am bad? As I pulled my nightie down, I started to cry.

"Shhh, don't cry," he said. *"You'll wake everyone up."* Then he rolled over and I knew I could go. I tiptoed downstairs ever so quietly and went back to Becky's room. When I got there she was already curled up sleeping. I lay there for a long time thinking and wondering what tomorrow would bring. I changed after that.

During the day I would hide, sometimes lying in the long grass in the field, sometimes in the hay in the old barn, but I would never tell. I wouldn't let anyone know the secrets of the night. Then, after a few months, I heard the news; we were moving far, far away and my heart was so happy. My dad, my rescuer, and he didn't even know it. I counted down the days till we finally moved.

Goodbye Green House

The house was going up for sale, so all of our stuff was put into the far rooms and soon there were boxes everywhere you walked. Our renters would stay on until it sold but we were leaving to go to Ontario so dad could start school. I thought it was funny he was starting school before I got to go, not realizing he did not mean kindergarten. He was going to university, Queens University, in Kingston, Ontario. He'd decided over the last few months that he wanted to be a minister, and the reason was he knew my mom went to heaven and he would do everything in his power to make sure he got there too someday. It would be a new adventure, new people and a whole new life for us.

Soon our little car was packed to the top and all our stuff was put in boxes, and I looked at our little green house and I said a sad goodbye to the good times and the bad times. It was still my home with the scary winding stairway, and nasty wringer washer. It was still the place where I cuddled with my mom on the couch and followed her around while she did her chores. This was my last connection to the places where I knew her.

Goodbye green house.

Goodbye mama.

The Logans

As we got closer to Kingston, dad started talking about where we were going. He had met a United Church minister named Dave Logan who had a young family, and was looking for someone to share rent. We were going to be staying with them while dad went to school. I was around six now, and very excited about the prospect of a new family.

When we pulled in, I saw the house. It was a stone house just off the highway and there were chickens and lots of other animals wandering around the yard. Then this woman came out and shook my dad's hand. With a great big smile, she looked at me and said, *"You must be Julie. I am Pat."*

Then she squatted down and pulled me into a great big bear hug. What I remember the most was she smelled of flowers and looked like an angel. Her long blond hair was tied back with a blue ribbon, and she wore a black turtle neck and flowing brown skirt that went to the ground. There was such a soft, gentle glow about her that I knew I would love her forever; her soul was kind and her heart was pure.

When we went in, I got to meet her kids. First there was Amy. She was my age. She had long dark hair and dark brown eyes; and then there was Jason. He had dark, curly hair and dark brown eyes, and when he talked, it was with passion. *"I need to eat Mama. I must have something to drink. Please, I need to go to sleep."*

It made me giggle just to hear him, but I also developed quite a soft spot for him too. He would be my prince in many of the games we would play. We ate then, and it had to have been something earthy like whole wheat bread and white cheese with fresh milk. Once we ate, we sat in the living room and talked. There was no television in this house. This was a house for the mind to grow with imagination and not with distractions like a television.

Soon we heard a loud booming voice. *"Hello, I'm home."* The kids all jumped up and started shouting excitedly, *"Papa's home, papa's home."*

Then this man came in, with long, dark, curly, hair and dark brown eyes that twinkled when he smiled. With one kid on each leg, he leaned over and shook my dad's hand, and he turned and looked at me. My eyes were as wide as saucers. I had never met anyone with the energy this man had in just a two-minute meeting; not to mention he looked every bit like Jesus in every Bible I had ever seen.

In two seconds, he lifted me up and he looked at me from arm's length and said, *"You must be Julie. I am Dave."* Then he gave me a great big hug; the kind where you let out a grunt cuz there is no air left in your lungs. This was our new place, our new family and I was happy.

Once our car was unloaded and we were settled into our room, I decided to explore. The kids were in this huge room filled with toys and pictures they had painted. They brought me in and said this was their toy room. There were stars painted on the ceiling, and the walls had trees and grass. Pat had done this room so they would feel like they were outside on a rainy day.

Then I heard Dave singing and playing guitar downstairs. We all raced down to hear him play. Some songs I knew, and we all joined in the sing-a-long; and with others, we would just sit and listen.

Then Pat said it was time for bed, so upstairs we went. She asked if I would like to hear a bedtime story and I quickly agreed. She told us stories about a dragon and the wildly incredible adventures he would go on with his friends Amy, Jason and Julie. Then she sang us a song of dreams; beautiful ones that carried all of us off to sleep. She really was an angel, I thought, as I drifted off to sleep.

We spent about six months with the Logans, and it was the best of times for me. There was a tickle trunk in the playroom with dress-up clothes. We could be pirates, witches, princes and princesses. The only limit to our play was our imagination, and we had loads of that so there was never a time we did not create different worlds.

Being how serious Jason was, it was very easy to torment him. Amy would never dare, but sometimes at night when it was time to get our PJs on, I would grab his top or bottom and run through the house with it. Jason would run after me, shouting, *"You must give that back to me. I really need my pyjamas."*

This would make me laugh even harder and run even faster until *Pat would say,* "Okay, now give him back his PJs." It was a time of discovery; even of earthy snacks like raisins, peanuts and sunflowers. There was never any stress. It was just fun.

Part Five

Dundas

Na'n

Our New House – the Manse

Once dad was done his first year at university, he could work as a student minister. The first place to hire him was back in Prince Edward Island in a small community called Dundas on the eastern part of the Island. It was miles and miles from Lennox Island and the green house, but at least close enough that we could go and visit more often than when we were in Ontario. The green house had sold to an American who was looking for a summer home in the rich, red province. Dad said he was going to bank his money so he could go back to school.

We took the ferry over to PEI and drove to our new home. As we were driving up a hill, Dad said, *"Look over there. That's my new church; well, one of them."*

There was the church on a hill so high, and the setting sun sent a beautiful red light over it. It was as pretty as a picture.

Soon we arrived at our new house. It had a u-shaped driveway, so we could drive in one way and out the other. When we went inside, it was huge. When you walked in, you walked into the living room, and there was a hallway to the left that led to the bedrooms. There was also a huge basement you could get to from the kitchen.

This was our house. The smell of fresh paint was still in the air and the boxes were in the living room. This was home, and first thing I did was pick out my room. It was the biggest, and the window looked out to the road. Our home was perfect and clean and new. There was a farm across from us and a house to the left of us. Other than that, we were in a field. This would be my world for a year and a half, and I liked it.

Chapter 66

Gary and His Sister

Life settled in and we made friends and soon, dad made a special friend. Her name was Shannon. I liked her. She had the face of a china doll and long honey coloured hair. We started visiting her more and more as time went on, and she had a much younger brother who was my age named Gary.

When dad was in visiting with her, Gary and I would play outside. Our favourite place to play was in the huge metal tub under the driveway. This tub was there to let the water pass from one side of the driveway to the other, but to us it was a place we could sit and talk for hours without being interrupted; that was, if Spiderman was not on. Spiderman was Gary's favourite show, so we had to be inside if our show came on.

We were the best of friends and I decided that Gary was going to be my 'second boyfriend'. He was funny and handsome and I figured we would always be able to play together as long as my dad was seeing his sister. It worked out very well for us and we were happy.

Dynamite and Frogs

Gary had a child's paradise in his backyard. There were boats parked, and odds and ends of stuff we could go through when we were bored. One of our favourite games was going on the boats and being sea captains. We were the best captains around those parts. Sometimes we would go on different ships and we would take turns being pirates.

One day, down in the bottom of the boat, we found a treasure. It was a box full of sticks of dynamite Now we could pretend to blow things up. We each took about three or four sticks and went up to the top of the boat. We were fighting ships then. If the other boat was a bad boat, we would hurl a stick of dynamite at it. It never occurred to us that this was a dangerous game. We were just so happy we could act like real fighters. We were the best. We were scary and had real dynamite to blow up anyone we didn't like.

Up the street, there was a neighbor who had a school bus; and whenever we wanted, we would go over there too and play school bus. I would open the big doors and let Gary in, and make him sit and be quiet while I drove him back and forth to school; then it would be his turn. I don't think any two kids had a better playground then we did. We didn't need to pretend for most of the things cuz we had it all there for us.

If we were feeling a little nasty, we would collect frogs and bring them to the boat and hurl them off as live bombs. No one would mess with us. We were fierce. Thank goodness we were never caught; our bums would have been pretty sore.

Chapter 68

The Murphys

Being so young, I still needed people who had big hearts to help look after me; and our special person who helped out a lot here was Martina. She was from away, and still had a thick accent from where she was from, but she was always so good to me. When dad had to go anywhere, she would be there to watch me and keep me company. Once in awhile, she would feed me yogurt which I did not like, but I did not want to hurt her feelings; so once she left, I would dig a hole in her fern plants and scoop the yucky stuff into the hole and bury it. Her plants, I think, liked the yogurt. They grew quite large while I was there.

One day there was a huge thunderstorm. Martina lived right on the coast. She did not like storms either, so the two of us started getting scared. Soon we were both packing up to sit in her car. She said it was the safest place to be if lighting struck, so we sat in the car holding each other, waiting for the storm to pass. It was so loud every boom shook the car from one end to the other, and the lighting would streak across the sky like fists of light. We waited and once it was done and the night was quiet again, we went back in for some more yogurt!

Church or Churches

When I was little, churches were not that much fun. You had to sit quietly and listen or sing, for a whole hour. My life at this time was three times the fun. Dad had three churches we went to every Sunday.

We would get up and do the first church. It was so early, I would be half asleep during most of it. At the end of that service, everyone would say their 'hi' or 'hello' to me, and we would leave and go to church number two. I'd be awake but the service would be the same, so I'd look through the hymnal; and since I always sat in the very front, I would sneak peeks at all the congregation to see how they prayed.

Then when the second service was done, it was time for the last one. I could almost say the whole service by this time. Of course, when the children were all called up for children's time, I was never allowed to answer the questions because dad knew I knew all the answers.

Once this was done, it was always a Sunday thing for someone to invite us for Sunday supper. We would go to one place one Sunday and have turkey and the fixings. Other places would have ham and some would have a yummy casserole. One thing is for sure, that when we were invited, it was planned well in advance. There was always everything you would want to eat there at each table, including desserts.

So, Sunday was hard but it was always the best of times. We got to visit, explore and eat like royalty. While we were there, the communities took us in and really took care of us. Dad's churches were his pride and joy, and even though he was still learning as a student minister, they treated him like gold.

First Realization I Had No Mother

I was in Grade 1 here on Prince Edward Island, and I liked school. I didn't love it, but I didn't hate it either. Then came a day I was not expecting.

Parent-teacher night was coming up; my very first one, ever. None of the kids knew what it all meant so we asked the teacher. She explained to us that parent-teacher night is when the moms and dads come in and see our teacher and our classroom, and she gets a chance to talk to them about how we are all doing in school. This made sense, but it also made me sad.

I walked home from school that night and went into our study. Dad usually sat there for hours making smoke rings and writing out his services, but he was away today so I went to the photo albums and took out a picture that I would need for school the next day.

Morning came and off to school I went. I knew it was show and tell and I wanted to go first. When it was time, I almost jumped out of my chair to be noticed. Our teacher picked me, and I went up to the head *of the class and said, "Tonight is parent-teacher night, and I want everyone to know that I do have a mom. She might not be with us right now, but here is her picture so you all know who she is."*

The classroom was quiet as I went back to my seat. The teacher had tears in her eyes when she called up the next child for show and tell. I held that picture tightly and just stared at my mom, with her long dark hair, sitting on a couch in the green house, looking so young and so beautiful. My mom, I can barely remember her at all. Her face was gone aside from the pictures I'd collected of her. Her voice was gone, like the sound of my favourite bird. I would know it if I heard it, but it wouldn't come to mind no matter how hard I looked for it in my mind. With that one event, I lost all I had left of her, and it hurt from the inside of my chest to the tips of my toes.

Unexpected Family

While we were in Dundas, we would travel out to Lennox Island about once or twice a month and spend time there. Dad missed his friends and family so we always made an effort to be there. One day we were out, and we picked up Philip and Darlene. Dad's plan was to take them out for supper and spend some time with them. On the way to town, dad realized we needed some gas, so we pulled over to get gas. While he was in paying, Darlene turned around from the front seat and said plain as day, *"Did you know I am your sister?"*

I looked at her, blinked a few times and replied as plainly, *"No you're not."*

*"Yes, I am, "*she said, getting a little bit irritated at this point.

*"Awe, no you're not, "*I shot back.

Then dad came out and sat down in his seat. Darlene turned to him and said, *"You tell her that I am her sister."*

Dad looked from me to her and back to me again, and said very fast and very quiet, *"Yes, she is your sister and we will talk about it later."*

I had a sister, a real sister, someone who was mine because we were the same. I had someone. She was my sister, mine. I smiled all the way to town, all the way through supper and all the way back to Lennox. It took more than a little while for me to understand that we had the same mom, but not the same dad. That made no sense at all to me. Maybe my dad wanted to wait, because he did not have the answers I needed yet.

I never pushed it. I was content. There was another person out there who shared who I was, who shared what I lost, who would be there for me when I needed her. The world was looking better for me all the time. I had a sister.

Sis and me

The Piano

Now that I was in school and getting bigger, dad wanted me to start to play the piano. He would look in the paper and ask around, and after a little while, he found an old player piano in his price range. An old player piano is almost the same as a regular piano except it has the ability to play without being played. You pump the two foot pedals and it plays a song. It's the same song over and over, but it is a song.

Dad had made a friend while he was in Montreal named Joe, and Joe was very smart. He volunteered to come over and take the insides out and make our player piano into a real piano. Well, Joe came and soon there were these lumps of metal with screws and shiny things all over.

I asked dad if I could take them apart in the basement. I took them down and spent days and weeks unscrewing every screw and putting them in jars; and finally, when I was done, dad came, took what was good and we tossed the rest. It inspired me. Soon I was taking apart my alarm clocks and radios and the appliances, and I would only get in trouble if I could not put the stuff back together again.

Joe took a job working on wind energy here on the Island. I would like to think it is his footsteps we follow with all the new development in that area now.

Beware of Yellow Jackets

As I did a lot with dad, we would drive and drive and stop and get out and walk. It did not matter where we were, whose land it was or what time it was, we would walk. These were the best of adventures most times. We would find little hidden streams and tiny waterfalls, fields and flowers, or hidden fruits like apples and strawberries. These days we always had new discoveries. We were true explorers.

One day we were walking and as usual, I was quite a bit behind dad when I heard a loud crunch sound and a yell, and then I saw dad come running through the long grass and right to me. He picked me up and kept running. He'd stepped on a yellow jacket nest.

He told me about it once we were back safe in the car and he was nursing a few nasty looking bites. Yellow Jackets are nasty creatures. They'll go after you just for spite and go for blood if you disturb their home as he did when he stepped on it. We stayed much closer to our car for the next few adventures, just in case. Now we knew they were there. We did not want to see another blanket of angry wasps coming after us again.

Ants and Worms

Dundas was a great place to grow up, but unlike those last places we lived, this time it was just me at home when dad was away. It could get really lonely. Some days I would sit on the driveway and watch the ants travel back and forth to their home. Sometimes I would count them as they came out. If I was really bored, I would pick each one up as it came out and put it in a bottle to relocate it, just to see if the ants could find their way home. It made the weekends go by when there was nothing else to do.

Other times, I would collect worms, dig them up, clean them off and see how many would fit into my little jar. Ants and worms were my play toys here. Once, and only once, I collected a jar full of ants and forgot to let them go.

A few days later the jar caught my eye, and in horror, I looked and saw all my friends curled up at the bottom. I knew there was something I would have to do to somehow, someway make it up to my little playmates; so I dug a little hole on the side of the house and buried them there. I made a little cross and said a little prayer for all those tiny guys. I stopped collecting them then, but I would sit and watch them for hours going in and out of their little nests all over our driveway.

But It's Only a Beer in My Lunch

One of my dad's hobbies was making homemade beer for him and homemade root beer for me. Once every couple of months, the big jugs would come up from downstairs and I could smell the sweet smell of my favourite pop. Once all the mixing was done, it was time for the bottling. We used beer bottles and a homemade bottle capper with brand new shiny gold caps. Once we filled our last bottle and put on the caps, I knew it was only a matter of time before we would have yummy homemade root beer.

One morning when those bottles were cooling in the fridge, I decided to add one to my lunch and take it to school with a bottle opener. As lunch hour got closer and closer, I could feel mischief start to bubble and ooze out of me. With a twinkle in my eye, I sat in my Grade 1 classroom and opened my lunch. I took out my sandwich and then, with as much oomph as possible, I took out my beer bottle and bottle opener. Some of the kids started looking with wide eyes and one even asked, *"What do you have there?"*

As I popped off the pretty gold cap, I looked at the group and said, *"BEER."*

The whole group gasped, and a couple went running to the teacher to tell her what I was doing. I took a great big swig just before the teacher came and took it from me.

"What is this?" she asked.

129

"BEER," I said with a cocky grin.

"I am phoning your father." she said. *"I've, never heard of a minister giving his daughter beer for lunch. I've never heard of it ever!"*

Then I was in the office, my legs dangling and my head down until I heard my dad's voice. There was a slight panic in his eyes as he asked said what was wrong. The teacher pointed to the principal's office. As my dad looked at me, I shrugged my shoulders as if I thought they were all crazy too.

Once everyone was seated, the principal looked at the two of us with eyes narrowed and said, *"Reverend Pellissier, your daughter came to school today with beer in her lunch, and what was worse, she started to drink it in front of the class."*

Dad looked at the beer bottle on the desk and then looked at the principal and started to laugh. It was one of those laughs that started with the shoulders shaking and the eyes rolling. *"Would you please smell this beer,"* he said. As the principal put his nose close to the bottle, an embarrassed half smile crossed his face.

Root beer, soda pop; there was nothing as sinful as alcohol in the minister's daughter's lunch this time. He then looked past us to my teacher who turned with red cheeks and left the office very quietly.

" We apologize Reverend, but you must understand how all this looked to us."

Dad smiled. As we left, I played with the shiny gold cap in my pocket and smiled inwardly. What a day! What an uproar! Beer in the Grade 1 classroom!

My Watch, the First Step in Being a Victim

We never really had a lot of money, so whenever I got a present, it was a very special thing. One day dad came home with a little box for me. I was bouncing around and so excited knowing that after supper I would be able to open it. All through supper my eyes were on that pretty little box, wondering what was inside. The excitement was incredible and at times, unbearable.

Soon we were done and it was time. As I opened it up, I could see a very pretty little watch. Inside the glass was a blue flower with eyes that moved up and down for the seconds, and the petals were the little hands that showed me what hour it was. It was perfect, so pretty and it fit just beautifully on my little wrist. I was so proud of my watch that I did not ever want to take it off.

The next day at school we were outside, and I was watching the big kids run around hitting each other and chasing each other around. I leaned against the school wall and looked from them to my new watch with delight; then, all of a sudden one of the bigger guys started backing up towards me. Without thinking, I raised my arms to push him away and then all of his weight was on me, and my arm slammed against the wall of the school. CRACK went the glass on my new watch.

"Get out of the way kid," was all he said as he ran away.

My Watch, the First Step in Being a Victim

Nkij

The tears started then as I looked at my present. The little petals were gone, the glass was all over, and it was only the little eyes moving up and down that still worked.

"Be very careful of your new watch," was what my dad had said to me, and within a day, it was broken and so was my heart.

One of my friends came over and said, *"Go tell on him. He is a bully."*

I didn't tell. I never tell. It was just another one of those secrets that got buried deep down inside. That night after school, I buried my beautiful flower watch next to the grave of my little ant friends.

Close to the Tread of a Tire

One night, dad and I were going visiting and we were running a little late, so we were rushing around getting shoes on and running out to the car. As I jumped in, I sat in the seat sideways and leaned my back against the car door waiting for dad to get in. He locked up the house, got in, and as soon as he put the little car in reverse, I felt the door behind me whip open and backwards. I flew out and under the car. Dad slammed on the brakes, jumped out and looked at me. I was lying under the car with my face just inches from the tires.

This was still a time of not having to wear seat belts, but I had to wear a seatbelt for a very long time after that. Strange as this was, for a few seconds it felt like someone was holding me as I fell, giving dad those few seconds to stop the car and save me from an awful injury or worse, death. This was the first time I felt my Guardian Spirit working for me. It was the time I needed her the most, and she was there for me.

Sandy and Bambi and
Little Grey Head

When we moved to Dundas, we had a big grey cat we named Grey Head. He was a loveable beautiful cat that put up with all our house moves. After a few months, poor old Grey Head just disappeared and dad and I were both very sad. We missed our little friend who would meow at us when we walked in and cuddle next to us when we sat down.

Then after a few weeks, dad had a surprise for me. He had been talking with the local vet who had taken two cats that were being abused, away from a home. He was looking for a new home for them. Dad asked me what I thought and I was so excited because now we would have two cats. How much fun would that be!

Into the car we went and off to the vet's. It was not far and when we pulled in, I knew it was the vet's. There was a goat on a rope and there were dogs and cats and sheep and cows. It was so exciting.

In we went and there were two small cats. One had millions of colours and was fluffy all over. The vet said it was a Turtle Shell Siamese cat. The other was smaller and had more dark colours. This was a Seal Point Siamese cat. The vet explained after all they had been through that it might take them a while to settle in and even longer to warm up to us. Dad and I were okay with that. They were beautiful cats and now they were ours.

On the way home, we talked. These poor cats had been through so much, and so had the both of us. Somehow, through some weird twist of fate, we had found each other. Once we got home, we looked and looked at our new friends. The Seal Point did not like me at all, but would hover around dad. The Turtle Shell liked me though, so we each had our very own cat.

It did not take long for us to decide on names. They were sisters so we decided on Sandy and Bambi. Sandy was dad's dark quiet cat, and Bambi was my cat. At bedtime they even slept with their masters, and only when we'd both been away were we able to sneak in to see them lying together.

Riding a Horse

Across from our house was a farm, and on that farm there were horses; big ones, little ones, thick and hardy ones, and slim and fast ones. Each one was more beautiful and graceful than the other. Every moment I could, I would spend at their fence and watch them running around on their land with a beauty so wild and free, it made me happy down deep inside.

One night, I was told the neighbor had come to dad and asked if I might be interested in learning how to ride. I think he may have noticed me, hour after hour, watching his pets with a hope that maybe, someday, I could get closer to them. It would be a few days away, but soon I would be able to touch one of them and ride like the wind on the land and become one with that majestic creature.

Before I knew it, it was time to go over. Dad bought me a beautiful red bandana that I wore like a cowboy and the cutest little jean jacket. I was ready to join the ranks of all those cowboys in my books.

Now, from far away, a horse looks more like a large wild untamed dog, but up close, they are huge. My horse's name was Bella. She was big and brown all over. First I got to pet her nose, and it was soft and warm like nothing I'd ever felt before; almost like my softest teddy bear, but warmer.

I was lifted into the saddle and our neighbor started to walk with the horse around the yard very slowly and steadily. Before I knew it, I felt fear. What if I fell? What if she stepped on me when I was down? My whole body started to tighten up. My legs dug into her sides and I slumped forward with my face in her great mane of hair and my hands wrapped tightly around her neck.

I prayed, *"Please don't drop me, please don't drop me."*

Visions of riding bareback with the wind in my hair were replaced with prayers of just getting off this horse safely. Our neighbour soon noticed my panic and helped me off poor Bella, who was probably as spooked as I was at that point. All in all, I had about ten minutes of living the life of a true cowboy and really, that was quite enough for me.

I still would go and watch everyday, but when our neighbor would walk over to see if I was ready to ride again, I would say, *"No thank you. Maybe when I get as big as Bella, maybe then I will ride her."*

Then he would laugh as I walked away, still looking every bit the cowboy with my red bandana and little jean jacket.

Salamanders and Snakes

Around our house we had window wells or dug-out areas around our basement windows. These holes collected rocks and sand and sometimes, if I was lucky, they would also collect little four legged pets for me. Salamanders are way bigger than the little newts I would catch in Charlton. For those who have never seen one of these little creatures, imagine a snake and a frog thrown together and what it would look like. They have the head of a snake, but with four legs and little webbed feet at the end of each.

The salamanders I caught were always very nice. They would never ever bite me. They'd run so fast it was hard to catch them. In the spring, I would use our big bucket and start collecting as many as I could, and then let them go when I got bored with them.

As the summer went on, I would be able to catch little garter snakes. They could be nasty when they wanted to be. Even the smallest, tiniest ones would still bite me if they did not feel like getting picked up by a little girl. Snakes, I would name after the men in my life. I had at least five Garys during my snake collecting days.

One day I found the biggest snake ever. It was going to be my most prized possession; something I could show all the women from the church who stopped by; something I was thinking of keeping in my bucket in the basement all winter as a pet.

When I reached in the bucket for the tail to lift out my newly claimed pet, somehow as I lifted it, it was able to curl up and bring that huge head up to my hand and bite. I let go of the tail but those teeth were still locked onto my hand, so I started shaking my hand, hoping that snake would let go of me. Then he flew high in the air and into the deep grass of our yard. The tears came. My pet, Gary the fifth, was gone and I was not going to chase this one. It had won its freedom, and I had much more respect when handling snakes from then on out; not to mention that, the bigger ones, I let slither on by!

Camp Abegweit and My Summer There

Being a student minister had some great benefits at times, and one of those was the time dad was offered a two-week position as a chaplin at a summer retreat right on the beautiful red banks of Prince Edward Island. It was going to be fun. Dad and I would get our own little cottage out there and the people would feed us and plan activities for us to enjoy. All dad had to do was lead services, say grace at meals and help out when he was needed.

This camp was called Camp Abegweit, and it was right on the shore where you could look out over the water and see Nova Scotia and New Brunswick. It had about ten little cottages and one main building with a kitchen and a dining area. Week one began with the kids slowly getting dropped off by their parents and assigned a cottage they had to share with another child. I stayed in my little cottage and watched as each cottage filled.

Ours had two bunk beds and that was it; one for me and one for dad. There was just enough room to store our luggage and that was it, but it was enough. When suppertime came, we all went into the big dining room. Along the wall was a huge buffet with all sorts of food for us to eat. We all grabbed a plate and loaded it up, and many went back for more.

Then we went outside and built a fire on the shore. There were already logs neatly set up in a circle for us to sit and participate in the singing and storytelling of the night. What fun it was!

We took turns yelling out songs we knew, and we would all sing the songs as loud and as strong as we could until the next song started. When I walked back to our little cottage, hand in hand with my daddy, I looked up at the stars, and even they were happy for me.

Every day was like that first day until Friday came and all the kids were picked up. Soon it was just dad and me in the little cottage again. The new group would be coming on Sunday and we would get to do all the same stuff with the new group.

During our alone time, I decided to explore the huge kitchen. There were shelves and shelves lined with giant sized cans and bottles of food. The pickle jar was so big, I was sure it could hold most of the clothes I brought with me to the camp. What a treasure that would be to have. The amount of "pets" I could fit in there would be fantastic Then there were the cans of soup. Having always seen the little cans we bought at the store, it was a shock to see these super big cans that looked like they were the size of my head. There were also boxes and boxes of cereals and other assorted foods. The kitchen was a treasure trove of food. Who knew there was this much food in the whole world!

Once I was done with the kitchen and dad was nowhere in sight, it was time to explore the beach. Down the little cliff and down to the shore I climbed, onto the red sandy beach. Then I started walking. Before too long, I came to a bigger beach. The red sand went out for forever with ripples of water going farther and farther out to the ocean.

It was near there that I found caves deep in the cliffs. Carefully,

I climbed in one and sat down. It was cooler in there, out of the sun, and quiet. There were little pools of water scattered all over the inside of the cave and in each of these little pools were creatures I'd never seen before. They were in little purple, pink, green and even red shells. Before I knew it, my pockets were full of these new discoveries and thoughts of all the things I could do with them. Then I realized I had better head back. It had been a fun day and I did not want it to end badly, so back to camp I headed.

When I got back, dad was still in his meeting and it was getting dark, so I went to the cottage. I could feel myself being tired and grouchy, so I lay down on my bunk bed and waited. The minutes seemed like hours and soon I had about twenty mosquitoes buzzing around me, all wanting to drink my blood.

As the time went on, I started getting mad. Where was my dad? He should be here by now. I started to plot. I would let the mosquitoes eat me up, and when dad did come back, there would be just a dried-up Julie lying on the top bunk. He would wish he had come back earlier and kept me company, so off came the sleeping bag. Soon I could feel them biting me on my feet, my legs, my arms and then my face. Then another thought hit me. I couldn't leave him; he would be alone if I was gone. The sleeping bag soon covered me again, and I tried to sleep.

A few hours later, the itching started, first with my feet, then my legs, my arms and then my face. I got what I deserved, just thinking of leaving my daddy, so I suffered in silence, scratching until the itches turned into welts and then open sores. When dad got back to our little cottage, the world was right again. I climbed down and cuddled into him, my daddy, my world. I would never, never leave him!

The next week was a blur of campfires, and one strange camper who would eat ketchup with everything. He would put it on everything on his plate and bowl, including cereal. All of us would stare in amazement at how he ate. Other than our ketchup-crazy camper, the days were always the same, but it was good.

At the end of the two weeks, dad and I were given special gifts. My gift was a green t-shirt with Camp Abegweit on it. I wore it all the way home. I couldn' t wait for school to start so I could show everyone my camp shirt I got from summer camp!

Hiding Food

Breakfast, lunch and supper were always good times, but could also be times I'd start to worry. Dad still liked to cook for an army, and it was almost always for just him and me. I knew the work dad did to make the meals and how bad he would feel when I didn't eat much of it, but with my tummy the size of a plum, it didn't take much for me to be full.

Then I had a plan. I would eat till I was full, and pretend to eat until dad was done and got up. Then I would hide my uneaten food around the house, under our living room rug, behind the couch, way back in the cupboard. It was such a great plan.
How could it fail?

Dad was always so happy when I finished my food. There was no way this plan could fail, until one fateful day, it happened. As we were sitting watching TV in the living room, the cat started scratching at the rug, digging at it and trying to get under it. As dad and I watched, the cat dragged out an old sausage and started to eat it. Dad got up and lifted the rug, under which was a mass of old eggs, toast and a sausage covered with white, wiggly creatures that tried to escape once the rug was lifted from their home. I tried to look as puzzled as dad over this whole event, but he knew and soon I knew, he knew.

All night we went through the house, to all my hiding spots, and we cleaned up each and every little stash. It was a sad chore. Dad did not say too much but would give me a sad, disappointed look each time I pointed to a new area in the house that I had used to hide my food. I stopped hiding food then and there. I felt so bad, not so much for what I'd done; it was still the best plan I'd ever come up with, but because I hurt my dad. That was what I had tried not to do in the first place.

The Lennox Island Visit

Once and awhile, dad would say, *"We are going to Lennox today,"* and we'd pack up the car and head out. It was a long drive, so half the drive would be spent lying on the floor of the passenger side watching dad as he gazed at the road; or looking up at all the wiring under the dash, and wondering how it all came together and what each wire did. When I got bored of that, I would climb into the back seat and lie there and watch the clouds out of the back window. The animals I could pick out; their shapes and colours were my entertainment for these trips.

When we got there, it was like coming home. It would start with loads of people coming out of grandma's and grandpa's house, surrounding us like a blanket with hugs and kisses. Then the kids and I would disappear into the house and sit on one of the bunk beds and catch up on the latest news.

When we were done catching up, we would walk to the store. It was always more fun when we had money. On those lucky days, we would go and pick out candy for everyone. Other days, when we had no money, we would go there just to see who else was there who might have money and candy. There was, like, an unwritten law. We all shared. This was the only place I had ever been to where this was true. If one of us had something, we would share. There was no talking about it, no negotiating; it was just how things were. I loved that feeling of belonging, of being included.

After we had our play, we would go back to the house, and if it was close to suppertime that meant it was time to go. Every time, I would whine, *"Why do we have to go?"*

"It is that time," was all he would say to me. Then, on the way home, *dad would say, "We leave before supper because your grandma and grandpa have a lot of people they have to feed, and we don't want our visits to be a burden to them."*

As is the custom with the kids, it was the same with the adults. If we were there at suppertime that meant we were fed; even if food was slim and there were many mouths to feed. Even if everyone got less, everyone got something. Dad did not want to take food, so we always left before supper.

I wondered if they knew that was what he was doing, and if so, what they thought of it. Did they appreciate that we did not stay and take food from the children, or were they sad that they could not share what they had? I never asked. It was one of those unspoken things; a mystery to me.

Oysters and Jelly Fish

If the season was right, dad and I would go down to the shore and stay there all afternoon. Dad would bring out his oyster belt. It had a space on it for his oyster knife and oyster sauce, and he would put it on around his waist. Then, he would walk out into the water and feel around with his toes until he found a spot that hid his oysters. I'd know because he would lean down into the water and pull up the oyster. Within the span of two seconds, that oyster knife would be out, the shell cracked and the sauce would come out. With a splash of sauce, he could lift up the shell, tilt his head back and swallow it whole. As I watched, my face would twist up in disgust. How gross If he caught me looking that way, he would catch the next oyster and start running to the beach yelling, *"Julie, I have an oyster for you. Come on. Try it. It's good."*

I'd run like there was a fire behind me. They were so gross. I did not want to be near it, let alone eat one. I can just imagine how it looked. There was a great big man, six feet tall, running out of the ocean with his big oyster belt on, chasing his little girl around the beach with his hard earned oyster in one hand and his oyster sauce in the other.

During the quieter times, I would explore the beach. Sometimes I would find shells; other times, beautiful rocks, and sometimes jelly fish, all washed up on the shore.

The jelly fish looked like a jelly mould at first, and then after you poked it with a stick a few times, it was more like soft plastic. If I was careful, I could pick it up on the dry side without getting stung, and create castles, and use the jelly fish as the awful sea creatures coming out of the ocean to destroy the kingdoms I would create in the sand.

Some days there would be more jelly fish in the water than on the sand. I would not play with live jelly fish. They could sting worse than a hornet or yellow jacket, so I knew those were the days I stayed out of the water. Jelly fish prevented me from swimming, but also gave me great monsters for my beach play.

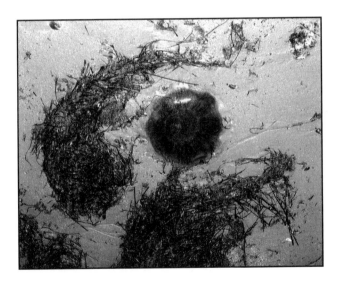

Rabbit Stew

There was a short time when dad would go out and hunt rabbits and all I saw was the meal of rabbit stew. It did not connect for me that rabbits were the real ingredient for rabbit stew. It was sort of like hot dogs. I knew that there were no dogs in hot dogs so why would there be rabbits in rabbit stew?

One time I went out to the garage to see what dad was doing and I saw two tiny, still bodies. Then dad started to prepare them. First he cut off the head and pulled off the fur, and once he got to the paws, instead of fighting with the fur there, he just cut them off and left it on. He asked me if I wanted a rabbit's foot because it would bring me luck and after that, it became a tradition after hunting day for me to always get a foot. I had many lucky rabbits' feet over that winter.

Once the rabbit was cleaned, dad would cut it all up and make us rabbit stew with potatoes and carrots. Until I saw the whole process for rabbit stew, it was great. Once it hit me that real rabbits were used, there was no more rabbit stew for me. I still took the paw for good luck because you can always use that, but I would not eat the stew anymore. There were a few big arguments over the dinner table about this, until we came to a mutual understanding we could both live with which was, dad would give up trying to make me eat it and I would not put up a fuss when it was being cooked.

The Night We Were Touched by Magic

It was a cold wintry night in Dundas when dad and I decided we had to get to the store. Snow pants and mitts, winter jackets and warm, wooly hats were all put on for our big adventure. Once we got to the road, dad stretched out his hand and I ran to his side to hold on tight. We walked down to the store and picked up a few things for the house and I picked out my favourite candy. Then, as we were leaving the store, the snow started lightly falling around us.

About half way home, dad stopped walking and started looking up. As I turned to look at what he saw, I could see the lights. Every street light and every house light left a bright white stream that seemed to be going up to the heavens. As far as the eye could see, there were pillars of light going up to the stars marking our path home. It was so beautiful and powerful.

We stood there and looked at the beauty of the night and we both smiled. Someone was looking down at us and wanted us to know they were there for us, then and forever. With glad hearts and souls filled with love, we walked the rest of our journey hand in hand, while the magic lights lit the way home.

That night on our little Island was our night and we felt special for such a gift of hope and inspiration. For many days we talked about what happened, and whenever we walked to the store at night, we would stop and look at the lights, but it never occurred again.

Saturday Nights, and
Smoke Rings from the Study

Friday night was our fun night. We played games, read stories, had company or went out for fun. It was always a homemade pizza night, and the only time we had pop. Fridays were the best night. We would laugh and just spend time together.

Saturday was a day dad had to prepare for Sunday services so most of the day he would stay in his study and work away. If I got bored, that was the time I would go into the study and lie on the floor by dad's feet and just watch him. He would sit, deep in thought, looking into the air above him and then after some time, he would lean forward and write down his thoughts on his notepad.

If he got stuck, he would reach for his cigarettes and light one. I would watch as he took that long first breath of smoke and if I was lucky, he would tilt his head back and blow out beautiful smoke rings that would glide up and slowly disappear into the air. I would spend hours watching dad do this until he would put down his pen, and with a big smile, ask me if it was time for bed.

I thought of Gandalf the Wizard creating smoke rings in wondrous shapes like dragons and ships, and thought maybe dad's next smoke ring would be one of those. This was my Saturday routine and it was good, knowing how busy we would be on Sunday. Saturday was a day of rest for me and a day of preparation for dad.

How Dad Wanted Our Family to be Better

Now it was time. Dad had saved enough money to go back to school for a year and it would soon be time for us to move back to Ontario and leave our beautiful Prince Edward Island. Dad and I talked a lot about where we were, how far we had come and what he wanted for us in the future. He did not want us going without anymore. He knew once he got his education we would never be hungry and go without.

He wanted to have a job that would give him enough money to be able to look after us. I did not want to leave again. It was getting harder, and I was getting old enough to know that friends were harder and harder to make as we moved around. I was seven now and I could understand what dad wanted for us. He wanted our family to be better and I wanted that too. This was our time of sacrifice. We were giving up our house, our friends, my school; and dad was giving up his job with the three churches that he loved so much, and having to say good-bye to all the good people who had helped us throughout the two years we were here.

It was another set of new directions. We were going to be on our way. Once dad was done school, we would have money and a place somewhere to call home. Dad wanted life to be better for us and I loved him so much for that.

What Did She Leave Me but a Toy?

As we were packing our stuff back into boxes for the big move, dad came in and saw my Panda bear on my bed. He picked it up *and sat down and said, "Your mother made this for you while she was in the hospital, so be careful of it and know every stitch was done with love for you."*

A bear, was that all she left me; no words of wisdom written down, no copy of her voice so I could hear it again, no hugs and kisses at the bottom of a card? Why would she leave me and not leave something more of her for me?

Dad shook his head and said to me, *"She was not ready to die. She made you a bear because she thought maybe she might be able to come home and play with you and your bear. It was a gift from her heart. Knowing how much you love your teddy bears, she wanted you to have one just from her, to remember her by as you get older, and to know how much she loved you. If she wrote a note to you, you would not understand it at three, and that is who you were then. You were her baby and saying goodbye to you would really have been too hard for her."*

So even though it was just a teddy bear, it was my teddy; my one connection to my mother who spent hours in her hospital bed sewing it together, stitch by stitch until she had the perfect toy for her little girl.

Who Was My Mom?

Who was my mom? She was young and strong and happy. She loved easily and was loved by her family, her friends and the community. Here are some stories I have collected from people who knew her.

When my mom was little, she spent most of her time with her older sister Cathy. They would clean house together and also get "punished" together, which meant they were stuck in the house all night, up in their room. Their only entertainment was to stare through the empty stove pipe hole, down into the kitchen, and watch their mom and dad play cards. Once in awhile they would get caught peeping down, and after they would get a scolding they would try so hard to sit outside the light so they would not be seen but still be able to see what was happening downstairs.

Suppertime was not just a time to eat what you could, it was also a time to bring plates of supper to the elders of the community. This was a time when everyone struggled. My grandmother knew that the elders of the community struggled more so, whenever she could, she would share her food. My mom and her sisters had to go out and make the deliveries. That was one of their chores.

When my dad first moved to Lennox, there were a few girls who took a fancy to him the moment they saw him. He was a young, handsome, French man in their community. One of my mom's friends actually went into his office and took the hat off his head and ran all the way home with it.

155

My mother hearing this went to her house and grabbed the hat and said, *"I am taking this hat, because I am going to marry him."* It was not that long after that they were married.

Purple was her favourite colour. She had a purple dress for her wedding, and when she was pregnant with me, she had a pretty, purple jacket to cover her round, full tummy. As a teenager on Lennox, she would gather with the rest of the teens on the wharf and listen to music. All the young people created their own entertainment. They would dance on the dock for hours, or until they had to go home.

Lastly, she was not afraid of death. To anyone who asked her about it, she would say the same thing. It was not death she was afraid of, it was the people she was leaving behind she was afraid for. She knew that without her, everything would be different. Everyone she left behind would have to find their own way to the past, to her culture, to who she was. Death was the only thing that could take her away from those she loved, and she knew this.

From all the stories of her, there is one thing that all say with a sad smile and that is that she laughed fast and loved forever.

As your little girl, I hope I will be the same person I could have been if you had been here; full of love and laughter.

Goodbye mom. I love you, forever.

Acknowledgements

My deepest gratitude to Publisher Larry Resnitzky, who with his daily encouragements and flexible deadlines has inspired me not only to finish writing this book which I started in 2004, but to believe that my stories might be enjoyed by more people than just my family. Working through the process of getting this book to print was exciting. Thank you, so much, my friend, for all your help.

I was always able to count on Graphic Designer Shannon Murray and Editor Nancy Resnitzky, for their dedication to this book. They were both patient and indispensable in helping to bring my manuscript into book form. Thanks to you both for your great work.

I would also like to give thanks to the Prince Edward Island Department of Communities, Cultural Affairs and Labour; as well as, Executive Director Susan Harris, Communications Director Dennis King and the Board of Directors of the Mi'kmaq Confederacy of PEI for their generous support.

Biography

Julie Pellissier-Lush was born in Prince Edward Island in 1970. She spent her early years there and in Massachusetts.

Writing this book has been a way for her to preserve her family history and Mi'kmaq culture for future generations, and to pay special tribute to her mother who passed away too soon.

Julie works with the Mi'kmaq Confederacy of Prince Edward Island as the editor of the provincial Aboriginal newspaper, Kwimu Messenger.

When she is not working or writing, she can be found spending time with her husband, Rick and their children, Richard, Brittany and Sean.